"Over the years, I have had so many questions of God. How long will injustice go on? Where is God in our pain? But my friend Jeff Keuss says that we make our spiritual journey through wrestling with the questions, not just getting easy answers. This book will help you live the questions. If you ask good questions on your knees in prayer listening to God, then God will speak to you. And within his body of the church, together we can transform the world."

John Perkins, cofounder of Christian Community Development Association, founder of John and Vera Mae Perkins Foundation

"Part personal reflection, part Ecclesiastes-like commentary, part Ignatian *Spiritual Exercises* for training in faith that forms a genuine life, Jeff Keuss's book displays the practiced wisdom and gentle realism that comes from having looked into the eyes of both idealistic students and cynical adults. Life is not about certainty, he writes, but confidence borne of a courageous questioning—a pursuit that is tutored by philosophers, artists, and prophets, and deepened by divinely inspired questioners in the Bible itself. If you are ready for a more authentic faith and a more meaningful life, then Professor Keuss is the right guide and his book is a good tool."

Tod Bolsinger, vice president and chief of leadership formation, Fuller Seminary, author of *Canoeing the Mountains*

"Many may desire a shortcut to navigate life's struggles, yet Dr. Keuss's words serve as a balm for those of us who are both answer-less and weary. I highly recommend this book to anyone who aches for simple answers or has a friend, colleague, student, or family member who has a similar yearning. Dr. Keuss humbly and wisely pastors the reader through t e into the awe and questions that arise from the presence of

Gus Peterson, director of convocati

"Jeffrey Keuss issues a f acute anxiety and alienation of our s summons is not a package of certitudes. It ep, and unflinching travel into deeper wonderment rust. Keuss sees that certitude is not a dialect of faith; it is r efusal of faith of a biblical kind. The advocacy of this book is richly braced with engagement with great thinkers and our best literature. This welcome book, wise in its honesty and daring, is an act of resistance to frightened easier formulations."

Walter Brueggemann, Columbia Theological Seminary

"Jeff has written a book that gets at the issue of asking questions in faith settings. Questions, and critical ones laced with doubt, are crucial to the development of Christian living. This book gets at that and does an excellent job of nuancing those areas well. Read it!"

Daniel White Hodge, author of *Homeland Insecurity*

"'Life is best shaped by good practices that build good habits for human flourishing, and asking good questions is one such habit, one that's often overlooked.' With these important words, Jeff leads the reader through a finely woven tapestry of biblical narrative, cultural realities, and philosophical foundations as he guides us through a journey of critical questions found in the Bible. Those who engage with Jeff on this trek will not only discover new facets of biblical truth and their relevance, they'll also grow in wisdom, a much-needed commodity in our day."

Richard Dahlstrom, lead pastor at Bethany Community Church, Seattle, author of *The Colors of Hope*

"The journey of living has a way of raising unexpected questions along its path. Sometimes these questions can arrest our momentum and confuse our sense of direction. Weaving theology into the everyday, Jeff Keuss helps us identify and answer questions that we need to consider. In a world of noise, the clarity these answers provide will instill confidence in our pursuit of God as we listen for what he has for us. And all along the way we're guided by a scholar/author who is modeling what it means to journey well in life."

Terry Linhart, author of *The Self-Aware Leader*

JEFFREY F. KEUSS

LIVE

THE

QUESTIONS

HOW SEARCHING SHAPES

OUR CONVICTIONS

AND COMMITMENTS

IVP Books

An imprint of InterVarsity Press
Downers Grove, Illinois

InterVarsity Press
P.O. Box 1400, Downers Grove, IL 60515-1426
ivpress.com
email@ivpress.com

InterVarsity Press® is the book-publishing division of InterVarsity Christian Fellowship/USA®, a
movement of students and faculty active on campus at hundreds of universities, colleges, and schools
of nursing in the United States of America, and a member movement of the International Fellowship
of Evangelical Students. For information about local and regional activities, visit intervarsity.org.

Scripture quotations, unless otherwise noted, are from the New Revised Standard Version of the Bible,
copyright 1989 by the Division of Christian Education of the National Council of the Churches of Christ
in the USA. Used by permission. All rights reserved.

While any stories in this book are true, some names and identifying information may have been
changed to protect the privacy of individuals.

Cover design: David Fassett
Interior design: Daniel van Loon
Images: under water kelp forest: © Tammy616 / E+ / Getty Images
   abstract oil painting: © photominus / iStock / Getty Images Plus
   night sky watercolor: © Khaneeros / iStock / Getty Images Plus
   abstract floral background: © andipantz / DigitalVision Vectors / Getty Images
   dramatic coastline: © shaunl / E+ / Getty Images

ISBN 978-0-8308-4565-1 (print)
ISBN 978-0-8308-7093-6 (digital)

Printed in the United States of America ♾

InterVarsity Press is committed to ecological stewardship and to the conservation of natural resources
in all our operations. This book was printed using sustainably sourced paper.

Library of Congress Cataloging-in-Publication Data
A catalog record for this book is available from the Library of Congress.

P	25	24	23	22	21	20	19	18	17	16	15	14	13	12	11	10	9	8	7	6	5	4	3	2	1
Y	38	37	36	35	34	33	32	31	30	29	28	27	26	25	24	23	22	21	20	19

To Clara, Eilidh, and Miriam, who continually
challenge me to ask deep and abiding questions
that point toward faith, hope, and love.
And to Diana for showing us the breadth
and height of wisdom and grounding us
in the soil of confidence and confirmation
found in the truth of the gospel.

I want to beg you, as much as I can, dear sir, to be patient toward all that is unsolved in your heart and to try to love the questions themselves like locked rooms and like books that are written in a very foreign tongue. Do not now seek the answers, which cannot be given you because you would not be able to live them. And the point is, to live everything. Live the questions now. Perhaps you will then gradually, without noticing it, live along some distant day into the answer.

RAINIER MARIA RILKE

LETTERS TO A YOUNG POET

It is not about a "return to the Bible." It is about resuming of the original biblical unity of life with the whole of our existence entangled in our time, with the whole weight of our late diversity on our souls, the unseizable matter of this historical hour undiminishedly present in our minds; it is about standing our present situations with biblical openness toward faith in dialogical responsibility.

MARTIN BUBER

MODERN MAN AND THE JEWISH BIBLE

We too often forget that Christian faith is a principle of questioning and struggle before it becomes a principle of certitude and peace. One has to doubt and reject everything else in order to believe firmly in Christ, and after one has begun to believe, one's faith itself must be tested and purified. Christianity is not merely a set of foregone conclusions.

THOMAS MERTON

CONJECTURES OF A GUILTY BYSTANDER

CONTENTS

INTRODUCTION

The Power of Asking Good Questions

J ust give us the answer."

That was the response from one of my students in an evaluation of an undergraduate theology course I had just finished teaching.

The question: "What was something you had hoped for in this class that you feel will help improve the course next time?"

I've been asking a version of this question for over thirty years as a way to gain input from each new generation of students. I like to take some of the more esoteric theological concepts involved in my courses and ground them in things that my students see as pertinent and immediate in the real lives they live every day. So at the end of each course, I ask them to tell me how I might make theology come alive for them. Most of the responses over the years haven't been quite as succinct as this student's one-line request, but some version of "just give us the answer" comes out at least once in almost every course I teach.

And who can blame my students? I get it. Many times I have sat in a lecture, a sermon, or watched a movie just like my students and wanted to fast-forward to the bullet points of conclusion, get to the plot twist, and then save myself the time of waiting so I can get on to the things that really matter to me and break my heart and the heart of others. Getting to "the answer" is often another way of saying "get to the point that matters" or "why does this matter at all?" Our world is a confusing, overwhelming place, perhaps now more than ever before, and our instant access to the pain and suffering around town and around the globe can become emotionally paralyzing.

This search for something—anything—that relieves the tension and despair of our age makes sense. This drive for answers is natural. Much of this book will address the form and reason by which we seek the answers in our life. In the search for answers to life's difficulties and challenges, we can find ourselves turning to dogmatism, fundamentalism, and numerous other "isms" that close off further discovery, deep understanding, humility, and the connection with others that is the real source of much of our search for answers in the first place.

This is why faith is not merely certainty and conviction in a belief statement, although certainty and conviction do have a place in deep faith. To find the answers our heart and soul and body seek in this life will require more than objective answers. True answers that will sustain us for life's journey require some messiness, mystery, wonder, and at times even uncertainty found in relationships with others and with God. The drive to separate answers from ongoing relationships with others—as if we can have meaning through mere conviction apart from faith that requires relationships and humility—is actually an ageless pursuit that fails time and time again.

In her masterpiece novel of the Victorian era titled *Middlemarch*, George Eliot introduces us to Rev. Dr. Edward Casaubon, a vicar of a small village in England who, rather than attend to the needs of his community, is driven to find what he terms is the "Key to All Mythologies." This scholarly search is a quest to find the one great answer to life's meaning and purpose, which he believes is located in the dusty books of antiquity. Focusing exclusively on the books before him, and not lifting his eyes and heart to see and hear the people God has given him to serve, is a metaphor for what George Eliot saw taking hold of society and church life throughout the nineteenth century.

As the Industrial Revolution was bringing with it the high value of speed, efficiency, and wealth as the mark of a healthy society, Eliot lamented the loss of what she called "the mystery beneath the processes"—the wonder, hope, passion, and humanity found underneath the fixed and certain objectivity that comes from rational answers devoid of relationships and humility.[1] Casaubon was an extreme example of this quest for disembodied answers to the neglect of the flesh-and-bone life around him. Over the course of the novel he becomes fixated on his quest for the ultimate answers found in isolation and rationality to the point that he is left alone.

While this was Eliot's concern in the Victorian era, Casaubon represents a type of searcher we see all too often in the twenty-first century as well. In many American cities we are experiencing one of the greatest US surges in homelessness simultaneously with unparalleled economic growth. The disparity of wealth, opportunity, and justice remains ever visible when I walk outside my classroom and look up and down Nickerson Street in Seattle. There I see people with cardboard "anything helps" signs being passed by Teslas on a freshly paved roadway, thanks to taxes from Microsoft, Amazon, Google, and other tech giants being used for building easier and more efficient ways to get to work.

The disparities go beyond the local, too, because as global citizens, it isn't merely our own neighborhood that drives the quest for "just give us the answers." As we turn our faces and our hearts to what's going on in Syria, Korea, Malawi, or Alabama, we face a deluge of images, data, and fierce opinions from everywhere on the political spectrum and reports of violence abroad and right here at home. To remember the shooting deaths of Michael Brown and Trayvon Martin and continued injustices around race and reconciliation brings us to the point of saying with a heavy sigh, "Just give us the answer!"

Regardless of who we are or where we live, the more we ponder the challenges that face us, the more we are confronted by countless passionately held opinions on social media, itself a ubiquitous and sometimes nasty arena where friends and family tear at, demonize, and polarize each other from their various echo chambers, citing pundits who get on the web to stake their claim as to who's right and who's wrong. Put together all the news, injustice, political noise, and social media mudslinging, and it becomes a flood—a daily deluge that can become too much to deal with. Our individual reactions and responses may vary, but the pain and confusion are a constant, and I see my students struggling under the weight of all the questions that they carry with them through our cultural blur.

A potent example of this is found at the very end of F. Scott Fitzgerald's first novel, *This Side of Paradise*, where the young protagonist Amory Blaine (a placeholder for Fitzgerald himself) returns to Princeton University, where he had been a student many years before. His life in those days had been filled with hope and inspiration under the mentorship of challenging faculty and spiritual guides, such as a priest by the name of Monsignor Darcy, but in the years following his graduation, he had chased after the American dream and lost his soul in the process. As Amory Blaine stands in the hours before twilight back at his alma mater, we hear these words:

> Long after midnight the towers and spires of Princeton were visible, with here and there a late-burning light—and suddenly out of the clear darkness the sound of bells. As an endless dream it went on; the spirit of the past brooding over a new generation, the chosen youth from the muddled, unchastened world, still fed romantically on the mistakes and half-forgotten dreams of dead statesmen and poets. Here was a new generation, shouting the old cries, learning the old creeds, through a reverie of long days and nights; destined finally to go out into that dirty gray turmoil to follow love and pride; a new generation dedicated more than the last to the fear of poverty and the worship of success; grown up to find all Gods dead, all wars fought, all faiths in man shaken. . . .
>
> He stretched out his arms to the crystalline, radiant sky.
>
> "I know myself," he cried "but that is all."[2]

I have read and re-read those final words of *This Side of Paradise* over the years. They have continued to fuel my teaching, my research, and my ministry to this day, and in some respects they are the fuel for my writing the book you have before you.

Too many people feel that the goal of life is to get to a point of clarity and certainty about their own identity apart from the messiness of trusting others and living deeper into the questions and uncertainty that life brings. Shakespeare's famous words from Polonius to young Laertes in *Hamlet* come to mind:

This above all:—to thine own self be true;
And it must follow, as the night the day,
Thou canst not then be false to any man.[3]

What is interesting is that when Shakespeare wrote those lines in the Elizabethan period, they were meant to be a joke or a laugh line of sorts, since it would have been considered simply absurd to base the goal of life on mere self-fulfillment. Hundreds of years later, to seek after mere self-fulfillment as the summation of life is no longer a joke but a seemingly noble pursuit. Yet as Amory Blaine discovers at the end of the Fitzgerald story, to "know myself" is not enough. Ultimately, the course of his life that led him to this conclusion is somehow wrong, given his despair in crying, "That is all."

How do we prevent such tragedy, the sort that ends with a despairing "that is all"? How do we counter this story, such that the ending cry of a despairing and broken generation can find direction and resources beyond finding "all Gods dead, all wars fought, all faiths in man shaken?"

One suggestion found in Scripture is this: *by asking better questions and learning to have faith amid doubts, we can learn to trust in our relationships with God, with others, and with creation over our need for certainty at all costs.* Through the chapters of this book, you will encounter examples of questions asked by people of faith in the Bible, and you'll glimpse how asking questions like theirs can offer a pathway to something beyond a despairing "that is all" result in the journey of faith.

Life is best shaped by good practices that build good habits for human flourishing, and asking good questions is one such habit, one that's often overlooked. Perhaps that's because we can think that the goal of life is finding not merely the *answers* but also how to ask sustaining *questions*.

I hope you find that to be human is to ask more and more questions, and that deep meaning is found in the journey and pursuit of where and to whom those questions will bring us. This is what Esther Lightcap Meek in her book *Longing to Know* reminds us of when she speaks of faith leading to confidence rather than total certainty: we can never have total certainty, but we can have a great degree of confidence and hope in our faith when it is tethered to our deep relationship with Christ and the path forged by his life and ministry.

Another truth vital at this point is to remember that if we're not careful and wise, the tiny moments of excitement that are offered by the latest technological upgrade, viral video, cultural craze, or fashion statement can, and often do, take us away from the core of who we are and who God made us to be in one important way: *they can turn off the questions before we've sat with them for long enough.*

What if the questions bubbling up in our hearts are those God actually *wants* us to ask?

What if learning to sit with the unknowns can actually make us more like who God desires us to be?

In our hunger to find answers and the weariness that often comes when we don't find the answers to life's questions in ways we desire—questions like, Who am I? Why do I keep doing the things that I do? Why do I keep hurting the people around me that I love? What am I so scared of all the time?—finding some tiny moment of excitement might seem like the only way to keep from going crazy. But what if God wants to join us in our bewilderment, in our sense of being off balance, in our visceral but unfulfilled desire to have answers?

SICKNESS UNTO DEATH

We're not the first ones to wrestle with hard questions and thirst for answers. In the nineteenth century, Danish theologian Søren Kierkegaard described our condition as a "sickness unto death."[4] As he watched the Industrial Revolution take hold of Europe—people moving away from farms and communities and into factory work—Kierkegaard began to sense that the very nature of a human being was changing. No longer were people living as fully human. Instead, they were starting to resemble something more like tools: pulling levers, shoveling coal, moving carts, turning cogs.

Akin to Karl Marx, Kierkegaard felt that individuals in society were ceasing to live into the full humanity of the people God created them to be: lovers, poets, farmers, artisans, thinkers, dreamers, mothers, and fathers. Kierkegaard thought that a shadowy, subhuman existence like what he was seeing emerge in Europe carried a kind of heaviness, a malaise and sickness unto death that would be, in a very real sense, the end of humanity, as the sorrow in their hearts would eventually grow into something so big, so cancerous, they'd no longer be able to escape being consumed by it.

We can see the same kind of heaviness in the eyes of those around us in the fast-paced twenty-first century. *If I work harder, if I build more, if I get more money, if I can find more success and more prestige,* we think to ourselves, *maybe then this "sickness" will go away. Maybe I'll feel more human.* I see this acted out in very visceral ways not only with my students at the university but also in my life as a competitive swimmer as well as a CrossFit coach and Level 1 Trainer to both advanced athletes as well as folks just desiring to get in shape. Driven by the need to perform at optimal levels, athletes will chase after cycles of dieting, interval training, and aerobic and anaerobic conditioning in order to achieve goals in performance. But those cycles can often spin downward without the insight and perspective of a good coach and a cadre of fellow athletes.

I have seen athletes forgo training with others and break out on their own for the convenience of scheduling and the allure of online programs. In these situations, it's not uncommon to see a well-trained athlete lose perspective and focus on unrealistic and ultimately harmful goals, resulting in dangerous diet choices, habits of poor form that result in injuries, and spending more time with a physical therapist than in the gym. Without the perspective of other athletes working together and the wisdom of a seasoned coach and trainer, athletes chase after illusions formed by memes on Instagram rather than the reality of a transformed and sustainable life.

Back when I was swimming competitively, I would get up at five in the morning to get to the pool deck before school started and also did dry land workouts after school with members of my team. Those cold winter mornings scraping frost off the window in order to swim intervals before my family even woke up was not easy. In CrossFit I work with individuals who are often overwhelmed by what they see in social media with godlike men and women throwing impossible weights overhead, walking on their hands, rowing with extreme intensity, and doing gymnastic muscle-ups on rings. But as a Level 1 Trainer I work with individuals to see what steps they need to make and how they can meet reasonable goals for their health one step at a time. They learn to be part of a class group that will give them confidence and the community to help them see growth in relationships as much as in their fitness.

In a similar manner, Kierkegaard saw his own contemporaries chasing after the performance goals of excellence in life. He knew that these cycles would spin downward rather than heavenward and that no amount of effort toward excellence, when done in isolation with illusionary goals, would actually deal with the sickness itself, and he watched those around him sink deeper and deeper into despair. Kierkegaard's own response, instead, was a resounding *No!* to the materialistic pursuit for more stuff and more prestige because it failed to deal with a very basic, core problem as relevant today as it was then: the sickness unto death is part of so much human life *because we have forgotten about God.*

THE WILL TO POWER

Kierkegaard wasn't alone in feeling that humanity was forgetting how to be human. Friedrich Nietzsche, a German philosopher and a contemporary of Kierkegaard, very poignantly said that human beings left in a world without God will give themselves over to what he called the "will to power." *Everything will be about power plays*, he thought, *every relationship, every job, every dream no matter how lofty and benevolent—everything that we do.*

In a world like that, people become mere flagstones to lay on the ground in front of me, stepping stones to trample so I can get to where I want to go. Nietzsche thought the church in Europe had abandoned its God, that it no longer thought it needed God. Christians were enjoying material success, church leaders were rising in cultural status, and the people who called themselves the body of Christ were living in a way that relied more on wealth than on faith.

Nietzsche looked at such a state of affairs and concluded that Christians had lost their appetite for God and instead only wanted power. His famous axiom that God was dead came about largely because he really believed that even the Christians didn't believe fully in the true God anymore, just a facsimile, a fraud. They had forgotten the real, living God they claimed to worship and instead sought only after power and glory for themselves. Where God may have filled their hearts once before, all of the glory, the divine humanity of everyday God-filled people, had been lost.

UNIQUE, UNREPEATABLE MIRACLES OF GOD

But here's the thing: at our core we are not children of darkness and loss. That's not our story. Every person that God has created from the foundations of this world is a beautiful, unique, unrepeatable miracle. That is a fact. It includes you and me: we are unique, unrepeatable miracles of God. That is who I am, and who you are. You are not a sickness unto death. You are not a will to power that's trying to run people over. But we can become these things—and because we know better through conscience, we usually start to despise ourselves for not living up to what we know is our potential for living abundantly. Thus begins a vicious cycle of shame, disappointment with the self, and a loathing of others that populates our energies, our consumerism, our conversations, and our online presence so abundantly and so fully that we can't even swat away the flies of the sickness fast enough, lest we drown in despair or sadness or purposelessness. It gets to be too much.

But what breaks us out of the cycle is the stillness that comes anytime we start to ask the essential questions of why we were made and who we were made for. We can't do that by living from one "brief, fleeting moment of excitement" to another by merely punching holes through things and walking over people through a cynical will to power. We need to stop and ask good questions, ones that will show us who God is and what kind of humans we can be in response.

LIVING THE QUESTIONS RATHER THAN "JUST GIVE US THE ANSWER"

This is a book about what it means to ask good questions—about how the ponderings and wrestlings that keep us up at night align with the questions that people in Scripture were bold enough to ask of God and each other. In a world like ours, where we can live an entire day deluged with information and social stimuli that we never even thought to ask for, it's easy to assume that asking good questions is like breathing; we'll naturally ask good, important questions about human nature as a response to the endless stimuli around us, just like all we need for breathing is air.

But as any athlete will tell you, there is a difference between working out and being an athlete. A person who merely works out from time to time will always struggle since training is not at the core of their identity. When I shifted from seeing myself as someone who just worked out to someone trying to become an athlete, I realized that my identity needed a complete overall. It wasn't just making room to get on a treadmill or to go swimming every now and then. Becoming an athlete means you are "all in"; everything shifts and you no longer think of working out but of *training*.

Athletes know something those who merely work out have yet to realize: no amount of natural skill will make you a true athlete. Only dedication to practice under the leadership of a great coach will do, and it has to be among a team of fellow athletes seeking to bring skill into a lifestyle of readiness for excellence whenever the challenge arises.

That's true in our spiritual and psychological lives as well. Far too often we can fall into the trap of thinking that asking questions is like respiration: it's something that arises naturally from within us and in response to the world we live in. But as any athlete will tell you, breathing is a skill that needs to be honed in order to be effective. The breathing we do while sitting on a couch reading a book is not the same breathing we need while running a marathon or swimming laps. There are short breaths and long breaths, shallow breaths and deep breaths, working breaths and resting breaths, loving breaths and fighting breaths.

So it is with asking questions: it's a skill and a discipline, and it takes time to learn how to frame good, life-changing questions in response to the many situations and contexts that make up our lives. In my decades of teaching university students, I have seen how learning to ask good questions has transformed their lives, showing them a world that goes beyond merely getting good grades and passing exams. History has shown that those who ask the right questions at the right time and place can forever change our world. Great questioners such as Martin Luther King Jr., Dietrich Bonhoeffer, Simone Weil, Howard Thurman, Dorothy Day, Shusaku Endo, Nelson Mandela, and countless others were masters of good questions. So too are the many figures in the Scriptures who grounded their encounters with their culture, their people, their context, and their God and dared to wonder aloud about the things they couldn't figure out.

These are people whose faith was forged in bold dissatisfaction with the status quo, tested in a fiery, passionate yearning for what *could* be, and ratified through their willingness to live brokenhearted in order to question well. Through it all, they showed us—they *continue* to show us—something about who God is and who we are to be in response.

A SHORT LIST OF DEFINITIONS

Communication rises and falls on people agreeing, whether implicitly or explicitly, on the meaning of the words they say to one another. As you work through the book, you will come across a few commonly used terms and phrases. Here's how I'll use them.

- *Doubt.* A willingness to dig deeper into truth claims rather than merely dismissing them out of hand.

- *Belief.* Acceptance of something as true or worthy of affirmation, not merely in word but also in deed.

- *Absolute Certainty.* The state of affirming no possibility of being wrong and of being closed off to questioning. Not all certainty is wrong. When certainty is part of faith and relationships it is life giving; when it is isolated from faith and doubt it can breed dogmatism and cruelty.

- *Faith* (in anything). The continuous act of believing in all aspects of life, and committing to someone or something despite occasional uncertainty, with a willingness always to be questioned for the sake of deeper understanding.

As you dig into the stories of the various people in this book and the questions they ask, be sure to think about the role that doubt, belief, certainty, and faith play as these people wrestle with God and others. Put yourself in their place and in their questions. Feel what it's like to ask the deep questions and be willing to rest in the uncertain moments of waiting prior to discovery and resolution. My hope and prayer is that the journey of faith directed by a constellation of questions will build confidence and faith rather than absolute certainty and certitude where "knowing yourself" is merely the end rather than the beginning of what it means to be alive.

I bring much of my own journey of faith into this book, as will be seen. I came to faith while in high school and was exclusively "all in" when it came to who Jesus was and is. On paper this seemed like the place to be. Yet being "all in" was akin to being enclosed and shut off within the castle of my extreme sense of right answers and false claims, yes and no, good and bad.

This passion for following Christ for many years closed me off to much of what God was trying to show me in the world and through my education as I went off to college. My passion to follow Christ with absolute certainty became more about digging a moat around myself to keep out diverse voices than building a bridge to cross over into the world God created and desired for me to engage and learn from. I wanted to get to answers about God more than I wanted a living, breathing relationship with Jesus. I wanted to learn how to argue rationally more than I wanted to listen humbly. I wanted to trust in what others in authority said more than I wanted to risk my own voice and heart. I truly believed that rationality, right answers, and pure objectivity were pathways to what I hungered for: love, connection with others, purpose, meaning, and contentment. I was wrong.

As I grew deeper in both my faith in Christ and the life journey God had for me, I found that living meant messiness, confusion, uncertainty, risk, and lots of questions that continued to open up more questions. Yet every time I put aside my need to be absolutely certain without a doubt, I found that I had to turn and face Christ with true humility and wait for guidance. This is difficult, and it is heartbreaking to put down our need for certainty and ironclad answers, but it is how confidence in the Lord grows more than trusting solely in our own understanding. I am still trying to live into this, and the questions posed throughout the book continue to challenge me, as I hope they will challenge you.

Each chapter is built around a key question asked by a specific person in Scripture. None of these questions alone will provide fullness in life, but the constellation of these questions will build resources for confidence and encourage risk to trust in whatever next steps your life may have. If you are feeling stuck in your life—perhaps in a relationship, feeling the pull of some big decisions, wondering about taking a next step in your job, changing your major in college, moving to a new city, thinking about starting a new ministry, or simply seeking to deepen your life in profound ways—then perhaps this constellation of questions will provide a road map of sorts.

Take time to dwell on the questions in each chapter. Read, reflect, and journal your thoughts. Go through each question as a spiritual discipline and see what God's response is to you as you ask the questions for yourself. Unlike Amory Blaine in *This Side of Paradise*, there is more to life than merely finding yourself. Asking the questions that Scripture puts before us is a beginning step to moving beyond a focus on a self and becoming a person committed to a life. A self ends in isolation, but a life committed to the journey of exploration, risk, trust, faith, and love finds so much more than a self in the beauty, truth, and goodness of a vocation for the sake of others, God, and the creation around us. We were created for so much more than a self. Good questions are one way to release us into what it means to move beyond ourselves and into deep and abiding meaning. I hope you enjoy this journey and the companions you will meet along the way, both in the chapters of this book and in other deep question askers you will meet in your life.

If you haven't gone to that place before, I pray that the pages and personalities of *Live the Questions* open your heart to the God who wants to be with you, to embrace you, and to help you find the depth of who you are created to be through asking the deep questions waiting to be asked. This is a call to begin the journey of trusting in this God with all of your questions.

Sure, the desire to "just give me the answer" will hover over your questions. But just as these people of Scripture did, trust that perhaps the questions will lead to a relationship of faith in ways that your desire for answers may not. Be willing to allow your anger, your disappointment, and your confusion to come to the surface along with the questions that Cain, Abram, Moses, Job, Nicodemus, and the woman at the well in John's Gospel carried with them.

Bring forward those questions that have haunted you, and begin a journey of setting them honestly on the altar of the Lord. In the chapters that follow I hope you will find space to discover the depth, breadth, and height of a life that moves with faith rather than certainty before the God of big questions, who has even bigger love for you and the world you are called to serve.

1

WHERE ARE YOU?

The Big Question

Wanna walk to, walk off
The edge of my own life.

SLEATER-KINNEY
"NO CITIES TO LOVE"

And I am afraid. I feel the fear most acutely
whenever you leave me. But I was afraid long
before you, and in this I was unoriginal.

TA-NEHISI COATES
BETWEEN THE WORLD AND ME

They heard the sound of the LORD God walking in the garden at
the time of the evening breeze, and the man and his wife hid
themselves from the presence of the LORD God among the trees
of the garden. But the LORD God called to the man, and said
to him, "Where are you?" He said, "I heard the sound of you in
the garden, and I was afraid, because I was naked; and I hid
myself." He said, "Who told you that you were naked? Have
you eaten from the tree of which I commanded you not to eat?"
The man said, "The woman whom you gave to be with me, she
gave me fruit from the tree, and I ate."

GENESIS 3:8-12

I t's possible, in fact, to read the entire Christian story as a question, one that begins in Genesis, and humanity has been trying to respond to throughout history. It's the primal question found in the heart of Eden, *the* question that God has and continues to have for us—and it's found in Genesis 3.

WHERE ARE YOU?

A bit of background: in the garden, Adam and Eve are part of a grand creation that the Lord God has put into play. As God is creating the stars, the heavens, the earth, the waters, the beasts of the field, the growing grass, and everything else that comes about in God's creation spree, one idea keeps resounding: in Hebrew, it's the word *tov*, which means "good." The creation is *tov*. The water: *tov*, good. Heavens: *tov*, good. Human beings: yeah, we're *tov* too, good. Goodness permeates God's action in all of creation—pours into it and out of it, pumps through it. As human beings and part of that creation, you and I are thoroughly *tov*-ed, repositories of goodness that God has simply peppered creation with from the very beginning.

Then the man and the woman enter the picture in this garden and come to the tree of the knowledge of good and evil. Though they are aware of God's presence, they start to desire a thing that they are told is not for them: the fruit of that tree. Then, rather than consulting with the living God who is fully present with them, they turn to themselves, choosing to listen to the craftiness of the serpent instead, who twists God's words of reality, bending them beyond recognition, to such a degree that Adam and Eve make a decision that causes them to trip, to fall, to cascade into a place where they do not want to be. It's at this point that Adam and Eve realize they've broken relationship with God, as we hear in Genesis 3:10 with the fateful words, "I was afraid." They are exposed, naked. They want to clothe themselves, to cover up their newfound shame. And at this exact moment, God speaks a question to them, the first audible question to humanity in the entire Scripture: "Where are you?" (v. 9). And in many respects, I would say that this is *the* question for humanity, all of us across the generations. Every question we have fits into that grand one: "Where are you?"

The Hebrew word *ayekah* requires three words in English, "Where are you?" It's like a supernova of light that God is giving them, a dense and compact burst of meaning, in order to show them something bigger than they could have comprehended at that moment because of their fall. Grace and the call to reconciled relationship are bigger than shame and loss. But doesn't God know where they are? So much ink has been spilled over the centuries by theologians and laypeople alike trying to grapple with why God asks this question. Does God have to play hide-and-seek? Really? The all-knowing, all-powerful God of the universe can't find two people in a garden that he made? Doesn't it seem kind of strange for God Almighty to say in essence, "Come out, come out, wherever you are"?

But the passage isn't set up because God is somehow ignorant and has no idea where they are. It's a rhetorical question, one that God is asking in order to create a space for Adam and Eve to admit that they have run away. It's like a parent who sees that a child has stolen a cookie from the jar. Fifteen seconds ago there was a single cookie left in the jar, but now there's none—just a child standing beside an empty cookie jar wearing a chocolatey chin and an angelic expression, trying to hide crumb-covered fingers. When the parent asks, "Did you take the cookie?" it's not because nobody knows what happened. Instead, the question is intended to give a space for forgiveness and repentance, to allow the child to be reconciled with the parent with dignity and agency. The same is true in the garden: "Where are you?" isn't a blame game. It's a loving opportunity for forgiveness, a bridge that God is building with this question to make a way to come back to a right, fully human state.

WHERE: LOCATION, LOCATION, LOCATION

As we look further, we can see that the bridge God is building with this simple Hebrew word *ayekah* has several parts. Let's look at this first part: *Where?*

Where is the place from which we will ask questions that matter. *Where* helps us understand the place in which we find ourselves by probing it for information and insight. Real estate agents will tell you that the first three rules of buying or selling a house are "location, location, and location." A property's surroundings are key when buying land, and location is also crucial when we talk about spiritual relationships. Where you are—your context, your station in life, and yes, your physical community—will affect how you understand who you are in God's eyes and in the eyes of your community. What we *say* about where we are also matters, and so do the choices we make toward where we are going.

I had a friend in college who had a reputation for being very truthful in the way he responded to invitations. Akin to Sheldon Cooper on *The Big Bang Theory* or the Candor faction in the *Divergent* book series, there are those personality types who prioritize an idealized form of truthfulness above all else. If someone invited him to a party or to someone's house, his response would almost uniformly be, "I'll be there as long as something better doesn't come along." He meant it as kind of a joke, but in truth he actually lived that way. He was always willing to say, "Well, I can't really make it because . . ." When an invitation to a better party would come along, that's where he'd end up going. *Okay,* I used to think, *he gets points for honesty. Maybe not so much for commitment, but honesty—yeah, okay.* My buddy's approach to commitment taught me about the kinds of questions he was asking with his life: seeking always to have an exit strategy and never having to commit fully to anything, as though he were always dangling his feet in the ocean from a pier but never swimming out into the surf.

When we tell people where we're going to be, or where we imagine ourselves being, it comes with the crucial dimension of whether we actually end up in that place or not, or whether we even intended to go in the first place. I got an email late one night a few years ago from a student who said she couldn't be in class the next day because she was sick. These things happen, so I emailed back and said I really hoped she felt better and that I understood that she had to miss a session.

Now, here's the thing about having a professor who also happens to be on social media—later the next day, this same student started posting pictures from a nearby ski area with her snowboard, having a great day out on the slopes with friends. The next time we were in class together, I just happened to have my laptop, and it was as simple as saying, "Hey, I want to show you something" and turning my laptop around toward her. "Looks like you had a great day on the slopes, didn't you?" I asked. We had a good relationship and had a good laugh together. I told her, "Next time the snow is that good, be sure to invite the whole class!" But I also reminded her that while I am pro-fun and pro-fellowship with friends, I'm also pro-truth. It was a moment of clearing away falsehood from the relationship between us, asking, "Where are you?" (or really, "Where *were* you?"), and hopefully giving my student a chance to reposition the physical and spiritual GPS locator to be more in keeping with God's intent for her and for our relationship. Similarly, "Where are you?" is God's way of inviting us to be restored to the fullness that God intends for our lives, just as Adam and Eve were experiencing in the garden.

RELATIONSHIP, RELATIONSHIP, RELATIONSHIP

In God's economy, the move from falsehood to truth is key to understanding that while our physical location does matter, we also need to align our spiritual locator as well. It is vitally important to know that God understands location not so much as *place* as *personhood*. It's relationship, relationship, and relationship—what we might call the *where* of God. Where we are in relation to God is the location of everything. Where are you in your relationship with God?

Two crucial Hebrew words dealing with *where* show up in the Old Testament: *poh* and *hineni*. Poh refers to a physical sense of here—as in, we are here, in this particular place, weeping and waiting for justice. But what God wants to do is to take God's people to a different understanding of where they are—not to dismiss the location of suffering or the cries for justice, but to focus as well on the relationship of God with the people present in such a place. And so the word *hineni* shows up, meaning, "here I am." Where "I am here" is a statement of geographic location, "here I am" is a statement of availability for intimacy and relationship. In essence, God is saying, over and over, even in a place of sorrow and torment, "Do you understand that I'm still with you? I'm still located in that spot."

Here's how that idea might show up in our lives: perhaps God is saying, "You may be in a job right now that you absolutely hate, but do you know that I'm still there, *hineni*, here I am?" Or maybe you're in a relationship that's a real place of struggle and you don't want to be in a place like that anymore, but really, "*hineni*—here I am—I'm in that place too, right alongside you." The grand question of God is that location is where God is in relation to us at all times. In this way we are reminded that presence with God is a full commitment to the question of God's *where*. Are we located relationally with God in what we do and what we say? Do we ask our questions of God from a distance or from a place of closeness and vulnerability? Are you willing to get close and intimate when you ask these questions and to let God respond in the same way?

THE TETHERED SELF

The idea of getting close to God, or really to anyone at all, might be a dying art in the Western world. A thought experiment I've adapted from MIT psychologist Sherry Turkle's article "Always-On/Always-On-You: The Tethered Self" will help to illustrate this. Imagine that you step onto a crowded city bus only to find yourself wedged in a seat between two people you've never seen before. Bodily, you may be in very close proximity to them, giving an initial sense of closeness. But as you pull your smartphone out to start texting and surfing, and as the strangers next to you do the same, a distance emerges between you and the people on either side. From this moment, you've come to be thousands of miles away from either one of them psychologically and spiritually, just as they've become from you. Your elbow might be pressed against his ribs, and the scent of her shampoo might be wafting into your nostrils, but online, you're texting a friend across town while one of your seatmates is doing a status update for his Instagram story, and the other is lobbing political grenades on a polarizing social media comment stream with an obscure relative in Denver.

The phenomenon of close-but-far is what Turkle calls the "tethered self," as though our *real* self is tethered to the social media stratosphere and we are pulled away and distanced from those who are in close physical proximity to us at a given moment. Tethering goes beyond distraction; it's as though we're living in multiple locations at the same time and fully present in none of them, living fractured, fragmented lives in different places and pockets all at once. I'm a fan of social media, and I find it connects people in wonderful ways we couldn't have fathomed even a generation ago. But when we become distant and removed from one another, when we can't actually be in the same space with another human and ask a deep and abiding question, then our true location is lost, and all that's left is a tethered fraction of the whole human person.[1]

ARE: TRUE IDENTITY IS A VERB THAT NEEDS FEEDING

This leads us to the second part of God's question: "Where *are* you?" *Are* is a verb of being. Anything that is action requires fuel, and so this part of God's question itself raises additional questions around who and what it is that feeds our ultimate questions. *What are you feeding on right now?* What are you drawing your strength from to ask the questions that frame you into the person that God would have you to be? What sources are you drawing from in order to see God more fully? What situations in life are acting as catalysts to help you to understand your *are* and God's *are* more clearly than before?

In the Genesis narrative the word *human* (Hebrew *adam*, sometimes translated as the name *Adam*) is related to the word for dusty, of the dirt, or of the ground (*adamah*). In other words, human beings are created by God scooping the created matter and blowing divine breath into us and animating us in the image and likeness of God. It's a moment of agitation, of crisis—God interrupting the status quo of lifeless dirt and making it move in ways it hadn't before. Similarly, it's often the crises of life that help us to refine our understanding of our *are* and God's *are*. In Adam's case, God's causing a crisis by scooping the dirt meant that Adam was still bound to creation as a dusty person—and so are we.

As people who are created out of the dirt, we are "grounded," bound to the soil and the created world around us. Just like many trees and plants, we draw nutrients from being grounded in the places and spaces where we're located and with other grounded creatures (such as relationships with other humans) that surround us, and we need those nutrients to grow. Moments of crisis show us where those nutrients are coming from and whether they're sufficient for our need. A marriage falls apart, you lose your job, you don't get into graduate school, you get a diagnosis that blows your world apart, a friend you trusted for many years betrays you, a new financial debt comes over your head and begins crushing you under its weight—moments of crisis like these stop us in our tracks. Sometimes we cease to be able even to function. In all cases, we have to ask what sources of energy and joy are going to sustain us through whatever is going wrong. What holds us up? Who is there for us? What were we feeding on beforehand to sustain us?

Years ago, when I was in college, I was going through an incredibly difficult time. My family was being torn apart by a number of things—financial troubles, marriages in shambles—and I found that the things I was drawing my strength and supply from were not sufficient for the crises I was facing in my family life. I was feeling empty inside. It was really confusing for me because I had been doing all the "right" things: I was active in Christian leadership, I was doing my devotions, I was attending a Christian university and hanging out with other believers. But in truth, even though I was nominally plugged in, it wasn't actually very deep, not very grounded.

I had convinced myself that a paint-by-numbers approach was enough, that I could just do the basics as other people did and everything would be fine. It was a life of shallow roots, and it wasn't sufficient for the storm that hit me. I believed intellectually in the truth of God's providence, but it hadn't sunk its roots into my heart, and it certainly wasn't showing forth in how I was living. So when my family crises started hitting, I found myself falling apart. I felt frantic, lost, angry, and disappointed, and I didn't know where all the emotions were coming from. It was as if there was a riot inside me, and I didn't know why it was happening or how to quell it.

One day during my season of tumult, I was walking across campus feeling completely at my wits' end, as if I was on the verge of being crushed under the weight of it all, holding myself together by sheer force like Nietzsche's "will to power"—when suddenly I saw one of my mentors coming toward me along the sidewalk. Steve was one of those grounded, good people, the kind of person who can ask "How are you?" and you know that he truly means it, that he's actually asking, "How are you *really* doing?" When I saw him, I knew that he would want to know what was going on inside me, and I wanted to avoid being truly seen and known in that moment, with everything I was dealing with—so I started veering to try to avoid passing him. But Steve must have known that something was up, because he corrected course, coming toward me in the direction I was now headed. Eventually, I knew that the game was up, so we met, and Steve said, "How are you?"

The reality, of course, was that I was awful—and it was at that very moment, when Steve asked me how I was, that the dam broke. All of the plaster I had put in place around my sense of emptiness, all of the concrete I was trying to build up to hold everything together wouldn't hold anymore, and I started to weep right there in front of him, in the middle of campus in broad daylight, and it was all because Steve had asked the question, the *real* question that I needed to be asked. His question, his simple "How are you?" cut right to the heart of the issue, which was that the nutrients I was trying to draw from weren't going to sustain my life. And I just wept. We stood there, and he was present with me and not distracted. At that moment I discovered that I needed to rebuild some things.

Steve helped me to understand that I needed new friendships. I needed to take my spiritual life seriously, not just as a hobby. I needed people around me who were willing to ask me really good questions and not let me get away by just saying, "Oh yeah, I'm fine." I needed real authenticity in my life, to be seen for

who I was and what I was really dealing with—to be known by
my true *are*. Through the journey that began with Steve's loving,
authentic question, I started to understand what I think God
was trying to get me to learn: that God was inviting me to grow
deeper into the soil of his love. I think he sent Steve my way to
help me admit the truth that I needed better nutrients to feed
the life I was called to live.

YOU: BUILDING A LIFE RATHER THAN A SELF

The *you* in God's question deals with who you say you are, who
others say you are, and what you want to become. Genesis 1:26-27
tells us that human beings were created in the image and likeness
of God, what we call the *imago Dei*. God's likeness is the core
of our identity and cannot be destroyed. Every human being on
earth is made in God's image—everyone, including heavenly
minded saints and wholesale sinners. (By the way, if you do a
Venn diagram of human beings, the overlap of "saint" and
"sinner" is found in all of us. Welcome to the human race, and
as we learned from the High School Musical movies, "We're all
in this together!") As repugnant as we may find some people, as
harmful as the crimes or morals of some might be, they are
created in the image of God just like everyone else. We are all
also made into that same likeness, and we hone and are shaped
by the Holy Spirit into alignment with God through our spiritual disciplines, through our practices of discipleship, through
worship. Over time, as we embrace Jesus' call to follow him in
daily life, we gradually become more like God.

But there is a tension in our lives because even while our
discipleship makes us more like God over time, we're often out
of sync with who God actually is. Paul struggled with this, as

we see in his letters. "I do not do the good I want," he wrote, "but the evil I do not want is what I do" (Rom 7:19). It is tension like this—the difference between who we *want* to be in God, and who we *actually* are at any given moment—that causes us so much pain and agony. Why do human beings keep hurting one another, in spite of what we know is right and wrong? Why do we keep doing awful things in the world? Why can't we do what we want to do? What's going on?

"WHAT IS YOUR NAME?" JESUS' TAKE ON "WHERE ARE YOU?"

But God wants to restore us to a balance between our image and God's likeness, as we see in an important moment in Mark's Gospel. In chapter 5, Jesus has just landed on the shores of the Gerasenes, which in Greek means *others*, referring to people who are far away from Israel. As Jesus comes ashore, he meets a man who has been chained, ankle and wrist, to the rocky tombs. The man is insane, possessed by demons, and people don't want to be around him. He's different from them, so they put him out into a place of death, the tombs, and leave him there. But when Jesus comes ashore, the man breaks his chains and rushes toward him. "When he saw Jesus from a distance," we're told, "he ran and bowed down before him; and he shouted at the top of his voice, 'What have you to do with me, Jesus, Son of the Most High God? I adjure you by God, do not torment me.' For he had said to him, 'Come out of the man, you unclean spirit!'" (Mk 5:6-8). It's at this point that Jesus asks him a version of the question from the Garden of Eden: "What is your name?" (Mk 5:9).

The question essentially means, "What are you known by in this world?" Up to this point, the man has only been known by the demons that possess him—shame, brokenness, deceit, anger, rage, vengeance, will to power. Those things crowded out any sense of the image of God in him so that he was calcified by the demonic names that were clinging to him. But in Jesus' encounter with him, and through the rest of the chapter, the Savior begins to peel the falsehoods away, as if to say, "*This* part is not you, *this* part is not you, *this* is not you, *that's* not you. . . . Oh! *There* you are!" The man starts to be freed from these falsehoods, these false names. They rush away from him as pigs rush off a cliff when Jesus gives the command.

From that moment onward, the man sits in his right mind, cleansed and whole, as the beautiful creation he was always meant to be. He is given identity and a pathway to life, to his true name, the name he always had, the name he was always meant to hold as a child of God. And this is what God wants for us. The grand question in the light of the new creation is "Where are you?" It is the big question, the one that calls to us over and over again, hoping against hope that we'll hear it and respond.

Where are you right now? As you sit here, as you read these words, many people have given up hope that they might find the true, deep name that is really there, like the demoniac found when he encountered Jesus. Many accept that the way things are now is how they're going to be forever. *I'm not really going to fall in love,* they think, or *I'm not really going to have meaning in my work,* or *I'm not really going to find a great connection with my spouse,* or *I'm not really going to . . .* a million other things. *It's just going to be this way. And I'm going to put forward a stiff upper lip, be a pragmatist, and work through this stuff because that's what people do.* Amid it all, they feel completely alone.

Church culture often hasn't helped. It's a crying shame that we live in a world where even in churches people believe that the goal of life is to be completely free of dependence on the person next to them in the pew: to be financially secure, to have everything they need, to be completely together emotionally. *I'll give you something if you need it,* they might think to the person beside them, *but I don't need you.* Not needing to rely on anybody else in life seems to be the endgame. And if churches are saying that's the goal, either implicitly or explicitly, heaven help us all, because that is not the goal of our humanity (1 Pet 2:9).

We are tied to one another, bound to one another. As we see in Genesis, the man and the woman are given to each other, and they are also made for God. There are no Lone Rangers in true humanity. Even Han Solo in the *Star Wars* movies had to find a way beyond being the name "Solo" in order to fulfill his destiny, and he was Han Solo! We need each other, we need the stories that each of us brings with our lives, we need our hurts and our pains. Someone needs your broken heartedness to show how a heart can break, and someone needs to see your victory over shame and brokenness to believe that triumph over despair is possible. People will need to see that you have ways of overcoming the problems in your marriage so their marriages can find success. People will need to see your journey of infertility so they can understand what it is to live in a sorrow that is deep and still survive. We need each other in order to become who we are called to be.

As we peel away the falsehoods and the names that have attached themselves to our lives like barnacles, Jesus will confront us with a call to find our true name, to shed the falsehood and lies, and come to ourselves in wholeness and clarity so we can in turn do that for each other. Because we are the body of Christ, each of us is more than a mere self. We're each a life built for and with others.

To ask the real questions in our hearts, to admit that they're there, is a scary thing. In her memoir *An American Childhood*, Annie Dillard tells the story of waking up one December day when she was seven years old and seeing six inches of fresh snow outside her Pittsburgh window. She and her friends decided that if it was snowing, and if there was to be no school that day, they were going to do what kids do best: make snowballs and throw them at cars driving by. In the story, Dillard and her childhood friend Mickey were pelting car after car, until one fateful instant when one of the cars stopped in the middle of the road and a businessman in a suit got out of the car and started chasing the kids through the neighborhood. The adult dressed for business became all-business in his chase, moving quickly with the kids through the hedges and byways of their neighborhood for blocks. Finally, the businessman caught up to the winded and out-of-breath kids and gave them a talking-to. But what Dillard remembers isn't so much getting scolded for throwing snowballs, but that an adult was passionate enough to chase them through their neighborhood and across their backyards on their own turf, and come close enough to actually make contact. Just the fact that someone cared that much about Dillard and Mickey's character development to leap into action and pursue them at all costs held her spellbound.[2]

When we think about a relationship with God, the ending of Dillard's story probably speaks to many people's greatest fear.

We're afraid that if God ever was to catch us after all of our running, we would merely get a lecture about all the things we've done wrong as our feet grew colder and colder. When it comes to asking the deep, transformational questions, many people are paralyzed by the prospect of God actually hearing and then responding. *What happens if I'm really truthful with myself, when I unpack the real question that's on my heart, with all its brokenness, shame, and hurt? What will God do with my vulnerability, my question, if I let God know it?* But because we don't want to risk God knowing what's inside us, we pack it tight, like a snowball. Maybe it's a little bit toxic because our lives have been broken and we're not used to receiving good responses to the questions we ask, so we throw it. Then, because we don't expect God to show up, we turn our backs and run as far and as fast as we can, like Annie Dillard in the story.

And yet, Mark 5 shows us that the God we proclaim, the God we sing of, the God we encounter in worship is not a drive-by God, too much in a hurry to pay attention. This God gets out of the car, puts on flesh, chases us with love—determined, block after block, to get to us, to embrace us, to let us know that no matter how far we run, no matter how much effort we want to put into making the distance between us, the *where* will be, "Here I am," the *place* will be the nutrients God can give us to feed our soul, and the *name* that God will call us is one born in love, with a face of joy.

2

AM I MY BROTHER'S KEEPER?

A Question of Responsibility

Once we are born, we begin to forget the very reason we came.

U2

"IRIS (HOLD ME CLOSE)"

*Some of us, white and black, know how great a price has
already been paid to bring into existence a new consciousness,
a new people, an unprecedented nation. If we know, and do
nothing, we are worse that the murderers hired in our name.
If we know, then we must fight for your life as though it
were our own—which it is—and render impassable with
our bodies the corridor to the gas chamber. For, if they take
you in the morning, they will be coming for us that night.*

JAMES BALDWIN

AN OPEN LETTER TO MY SISTER, MISS ANGELA DAVIS

For the past few years my family has been involved with a
program that assists with family refugee resettlement in the
United States. When a family is given permission to enter the
country as refugees, they are afforded certain rights and status in

order to help them begin a new life on their path to citizenship. This includes language tutoring, job placement assistance, and providing some basic financial support through government-issued coupons for use at supermarkets. Our family recently partnered with a young family of three from Afghanistan—a father, a mother who was seven months pregnant, and a young daughter—and much of our work was in helping them find a new apartment and navigate the complexities of government agencies, getting a driver's license, and assisting with shopping.

While many people are generally helpful and generous, one of the most heartbreaking parts of working with refugees is seeing how some people will make immediate judgments about them based on their status as refugees. As we worked to find them an apartment, some places would not consider them as tenants even though they had a guaranteed stipend for housing. When we assisted them in shopping, the stores would be very particular about what the food coupons could be used for, and it was a trial just figuring out how to buy some cheese and milk. These are people fleeing horrific terrors and often experiencing the death of loved ones in war-torn areas. They are people with dreams, aspirations, and hope for a better life. Most refugees have had education and careers and therefore are not adverse to hard work. Yet because they come from another culture and country and are getting support in their time of transition, this means to some people that they are not "one of us," which makes even the simplest tasks difficult and daunting.

After the Eid al-Fitr celebration at the end of Ramadan, which is the Islamic holy month of fasting (or sawm), the family asked to make all the support team an Afghan meal as a way of thanks. We gathered together during a hot summer day with all our children running through the sprinkler while we sat together at a common table enjoying an amazing meal together. We talked about how hard toddlers can be sometimes, the beauty of the garden we were sitting in, the spices used to season the chicken, and the excitement we all had for this new birth that was only a few weeks away. Under the summer sun, sharing a meal with our feet resting on the common ground formed and sustained by God, there was this sense not of separation but of family: people finding joy in celebration of life and the wonder of friendship. I wished that some of the apartment owners, the supermarket workers, and the government agents could see this moment because rather than seeing a statistic or a political issue, there would be recognition of common humanity.

If God's big question to us is "Where are you?" then how do we start to discern where we are? Can even the questions we choose to carry with us show us something about our "location" —how we relate—in regard to God and those around us?

As soon as humanity leaves Eden, questions begin to flow like a river seeking the ocean. One of the first questions recorded in the Bible is asked by Cain, one of the first children of Adam and Eve and therefore one of the first in a long, long line of humans to ask questions of God. Next to Adam and Eve, Cain is the first person in Scripture to seek understanding of where he is in relation to God's "Where are you?" question.

After the fall in Genesis 3, humanity had left Eden behind them, but God had not left humanity. To ask deep questions often presupposes that there is someone who not only hears but also has the capacity to respond. That's what makes asking questions such a vital part of what it means to be a human being: *to ask big questions is to admit that we are not alone in the world* and that someone else holds what we need in order to become more of what we are created to be. As the man and the woman turn their faces toward the world outside Eden, they're not traveling to an empty, forsaken place. They'll be journeying with each other, and with their Creator.

The good news is that humans were never left to work out their own survival, let alone salvation, in isolation from God or from each other. At the start of Genesis 4, a binding agent continues to hold human to human in intimacy, as well as human to God. "Now the man [adam] knew [yada] his wife Eve, and she conceived and bore Cain . . . 'with the help of the LORD'" (Gen 4:1). This "knowing" of the man and woman with the help of the Lord is deeper and more profound than just biological conception. It's the passing on of the divine spark of the *imago Dei*, the image of God, through God's constant presence and preservation of life— life with the potential for intimacy, connection, memory, and hope, more than mere survival day after day.

As we move further into the story of Cain and his brother Abel, it is vital to remember that Cain and Abel are already "known" by God and each other. In the very sinew of their bodies, they have been gifted with God's knowledge and chosenness. It comes in part through their identity, which is found in the family they come from: they are children of the same Adam and Eve who *knew* God and *knew* each other.

"Human personal relations," writes philosopher-theologian Dallas Willard,

> cannot be separated from the body; and, on the other hand,
> the body cannot be understood apart from human relations. It
> is essentially social. Therefore our bodies are forever a part of

our identities as persons. I, for example, will forever be the son of Maymie Joyce Lindesmith and Albert Alexander Willard. My body came from God through them, and they provided a social and spiritual context that, more than anything else, makes me the person I am.

Equally importantly, it is the body *from which* we live. . . . We do not live by will alone. Thank goodness! Our choices, as they settle into character . . . are "farmed out" or "outsourced" to our body in its social context.[1]

This body that Cain and Abel bring into their relationship with each other and with God is spoken of in the New Testament too when Jesus describes the nature of the kingdom of God as similar to the relationship between a branch and a vine.

I am the true vine, and my Father is the vinegrower. He removes every branch in me that bears no fruit. Every branch that bears fruit he prunes to make it bear more fruit. You have already been cleansed by the word that I have spoken to you. Abide in me as I abide in you. Just as the branch cannot bear fruit by itself unless it abides in the vine, neither can you unless you abide in me. I am the vine, you are the branches. Those who abide in me and I in them bear much fruit, because apart from me you can do nothing." (Jn 15:1-5)

Many of Jesus' analogies of the kingdom of God bring us back to the garden, reminding us how fertile the earth can be when seeds of grace are sown and lilies of the fields and birds of the earth continue to testify to the truth that we are still tied to God's providence and provision. When Jesus says, "I am the vine, you are the branches," he is showing us that we are each the body of Christ together, branches of the same vine. Drawing our strength and hope from rootedness in Jesus' provision, we are not only fruit bearers for those around us, but we are deeply related to one another. The point where a vine ends and a branch begins on a healthy, growing plant cannot be determined. They are truly one in body and purpose. Yet once a branch begins to wither, it's easy to see where the living plant is and where death is taking over. In life there is seamless unity; in death there is separation.

These agricultural illustrations are more than metaphors as we turn again to the story of Cain and Abel. As we shall see, the question that Cain puts before God is a question of separation, of life and death. It's ultimately about the effect that being connected through our bodies to one another as fellow humans has on our sense of purpose and meaning.

GOD'S RESPONSE TO US AND OUR RESPONSE TO GOD

"A man entirely unconcerned with his self is dead," wrote Rabbi Abraham Heschel.

A man exclusively concerned with his self is a beast. The mark of distinction from the beast as well as the index of maturity is the tridimensionality [concern for self, fellow human beings, and the Holy] of man's concern. The child becomes human, not by discovering the environment which includes things and other selves, but by becoming sensitive to the interests of other selves. Human is he who is concerned with other selves. Man is a being that can never be self-sufficient, not only by what he must take in but also by what he must give out. A stone is self-sufficient, man is self-surpassing. Always in need of other beings to give himself to, man cannot even be in accord with his own self unless he serves something beyond himself. . . . A vital requirement of human life is transitive concern, a regard for others, in addition to a reflexive concern, an intense regard for itself.[2]

The story of Cain and Abel revolves around the offerings that the two brothers give to God. In the narrative of Genesis 4, we are told that Abel brings an offering that has grown from the ground, while Cain has brought offerings of animals.

> Now Abel was a keeper of sheep, and Cain a tiller of the ground. In the course of time Cain brought to the LORD an offering of the fruit of the ground, and Abel for his part brought of the firstlings of his flock, their fat portions. And the LORD had regard for Abel and his offering, but for Cain and his offering he had no regard. So Cain was very angry, and his countenance fell. (Gen 4:2-5)

We are given no rationale for why God accepts the offering of Abel and not the offering of Cain, and in many respects, to ask that question instead of other questions might be part of the problem. "No explanation is given in the text of God's preference [regarding the offerings themselves]," wrote biblical scholar R. N. Whybray, "and it is not probable that the story, at any rate in its present form, reflects an age-old rivalry between pastoralists and farmers."[3] In short, this is not a story about whether God prefers a certain form of offering, as if God is on a paleo diet and prefers animal protein over grains. Rather, the story has more to do with the heart, soul, and "countenance" (Gen 4:5) of the one who is making the offering.

Abel and Cain return the results of their work to God as offerings shaped by their hearts and hands, and it is the intention behind each brother's act of shaping that the narrative is drawing out for us. In the Hebrew, we find that Abel is *ro'eh*, which is commonly translated as a "keeper" of sheep (Gen 4:2), as in an attendant or companion, which could be seen as a play on words with the later question, "Am I my brother's keeper?" In this way Abel's care for his offering is like that of an attendant in a wedding party, such as a best man or a maid of honor. In contrast, Cain is a tiller of the ground, which in the Hebrew is one who is *'avad*, a servant or worshiper of that which he is attentive to, which in this case is of the ground or the *adamah/'apar*. You may remember that phrase from the introduction as the dust and dirt we are made of, and it's also what the serpent is cursed to feed on (Gen 3:14).

Now the difference between the two men's offerings is coming into view. Abel is standing with God's creatures, who are alive and animated with God's power of life. He is attending to them as a person standing with the bride and groom, providing witness and testimony to "what God has joined together" in creation (compare Mt 19:6; Mk 10:9), all of which is pointing to God's work. On the other hand, Cain is not so much in a posture of attending and giving witness (*ro'eh*) but serving the dirt of the ground to the point of worship (*'avad*). Therefore, we learn something about the GPS location of his heart and soul: turning his gaze in worship to the ground is in many respects the raw stuff of human will. Whereas Abel's heart is ready to support the true bride joining with the true groom, Cain has focused his gaze upon the bride of his offering and worships *it*, and the work he himself has put into bringing the offering forth rather than the God of the universe. Abel is freely giving that which he is attending to, while Cain wants credit for his work in bringing the bride to the altar in the first place.

This is an important point to underscore and remember as we move into Cain's big question to God. It isn't the content of the offering that God calls into question: it's the respective relationships that Cain and Abel have toward their offerings and their motivation for bringing the offering forth in the first place. When we offer our gifts and sacrifices, including our very selves, to God, do we see the things that we are offering—be they plant, animal, or livelihood—as a representation of the image of God, who is to be worshiped as the Creator of all (Abel as *ro'eh*/attendant)? Or do we see our work and offering as the end and summation of all things (Cain as *'avad*/worshiper of the *adamah*/earth)?

John Calvin said that in the end, human beings have the potential to become factories of idols, in that we are so intentionally created for worship that we will create our own idols to love and adore if left to our own devices. Therein lies our downfall, he said, if we are not attentive to the creator of all things as the true author and perfecter of faith (compare Heb 12:2).[4]

In this way, Genesis 4:7 is the fulcrum and lever by which the weight of the story of Cain and Abel moves. When God acknowledges Cain's disappointment in not having his offering accepted, the Lord of life points Cain to an important principle: "If you do well, will you not be accepted?" the Lord asks. "And if you do not do well, sin is lurking at the door; its desire is for you, but you must master it" (Gen 4:7).

To be human is not only to be given opportunities for great joy and fulfillment but also to face seasons of grave sorrow and disappointment. To borrow a phrase from the Dread Pirate

Roberts in *The Princess Bride*, "anyone who says differently is selling something." Nowhere in Scripture does God deny or sugarcoat the reality of the challenges we will face in this life. We will be met with sorrows, heartbreak, and loneliness. How will we respond to such times? This is the issue that God is putting before Cain at this point in the narrative. "Rejection, no matter how old one is," writes Dallas Willard,

> is a sword thrust to the soul that has literally killed many. Western culture is, largely unbeknown to itself, a culture of rejection. This is one of the irresistible effects of what is called "modernity," and it deeply affects the concrete forms Christian institutions take in our time. It seeps into our souls and is a deadly enemy to spiritual formation in Christ.[5]

When faced with heartbreak and disappointment, will we run and hide from God and each other as the man and woman did in Genesis 3? How will we handle the reality that sin in our world swirls around us like a tempest, forever beckoning us like Sirens to choose our own willpower, our own self-delusion, our own point of reference as the definitive point of reference for all things instead of the comfort and insights of God and others? That's what God is asking Cain to consider when he challenges him to remember that sin is constantly lurking at the doorstep. We all need strategies for mastering sin in our lives, and it is better to be prepared than to be caught unaware.

I have a large chocolate Labrador retriever named Seamus, who tends to be passionate about very few things. One big exception is his food, which we keep in our laundry room. In the morning when our family wakes up, Seamus positions himself in front of the laundry room door, sits at attention, and stares at the door as though he's trying to will the door open with his mind. As I am making coffee in the kitchen, I'll often hear some soft moaning coming from the direction of the laundry room and look over to see him peeking at me around the corner. He'll catch my gaze, then point his brown, wet nose to the door as if to say, "Look, see that door? If I had a hand with a thumb to grip a doorknob, I would do this myself, but you could do this for me—like, *now!*"

I sometimes marvel at Seamus's sense of focus and determination. Where he can sit and stare with crystal-clear devotion, my own heart and mind often wander and become distracted from what really deserves my gaze and my attention. It says something when my dog knows more about the practice of devotion than I do!

Learning to practice true devotion, to focus, and to put systems in place to avoid the sin that is "lurking at the door" (Gen 4:7) to distract you from what God is calling you to become is central to understanding God's exhortation to Cain. He was called to become aware of how destructive sin could be and to learn responsibility to tame the things that can tempt and deceive. We are called, through Cain's example, to learn these things too for the sake of our relationship with God and with others.

In the classic story of *The Little Prince* by Antoine de Saint-Exupéry, we find some examples of what it means to set boundaries for the sake of healthy relationships, along with the importance of taming the things in our lives that have the potential to hurt us. At one point in the book, an aviator crash-lands in the middle of the Sahara. After being stranded for a time, he is awakened by a little prince who makes an odd request: "If you please—draw me a sheep." But the aviator can't draw well because grown-ups discouraged him from pursuing painting when he was a child. Besides, the real matter pressing the aviator's mind is where this little boy came from.

The prince doesn't care to answer his questions at this point or to excuse the aviator from the task. "That [you cannot draw well] doesn't matter," he insists. "Draw me a sheep." The pilot relents and tries several times to draw a sheep, but it never comes out well. Finally, he draws a box and explains that the sheep is inside. The true sheep, he says, is beyond his capacity to draw, but at least he knows where the sheep is and that it's safe, given the box that surrounds him. The little prince is pleased and delighted.[6]

In another passage, an exchange takes place between the Little Prince and a fox that he comes to know as he is exploring Earth. After some introductions, the prince asks the fox to play with him. "I cannot play with you," replies the fox. "I am not tamed." The prince doesn't understand the notion of taming, and he persistently asks the fox what it means. Finally, the fox replies, "It is an act too often neglected." He goes on to say, "It means to establish ties."

The little prince asks what this phrase means, to establish ties. "Just that," replies the fox.

> To me, you are still nothing more than a little boy who is just like a hundred thousand other little boys. And I have no need of you. And you, on your part, have no need of me. To you, I am nothing more than a fox like a hundred thousand other foxes. But if you tame me, then we shall need each other. To me, you will be unique in all the world. To you, I shall be unique in all the world.[7]

So the prince tames the fox, and they become good friends. But after a while, the prince has to leave, which occasions the fox sharing some parting wisdom with him. First, he tells the prince a very simple secret, "It is only with the heart that one can see rightly; what is essential is invisible to the eye." And second, the fox claims, "Men have forgotten this truth. . . . But you must not forget it. You become responsible, forever, for what you have tamed."[8]

Much of the Christian life is about coming to terms with the dark, shadowy sides of ourselves, and also accepting that in this life we may never be totally free from them. St. Paul himself lamented some kind of "thorn" in his flesh (2 Cor 12:7), as have many Christians through the centuries. As the Little Prince learns, there are things in life that we must tame, and in doing so we also create ties with them and forever become responsible for them.

Such is the way of sin in our life. It is often the things lurking at the open door of our hearts, refusing to go away, that torment us. But we have been called to come out into the open, to admit that we are tempted away from who we are called to be, away from the responsibilities we have for others, and to bring those temptations into the light. By doing so, and with the grace and help of God, we can learn to tame and take responsibility for our lives and the lives of others, including our temptations.

At the core of Cain's story is a question of what and who we worship, our relationships with others, and what response we think worship will provoke in God. In this we find—as Cain will—that our vertical and horizontal relationships are deeply intertwined. This will have deadly consequences for Abel as it does for other "brothers" in our life when we don't see the interrelationship of who we see God as being and desiring and who we hold as our relational responsibility and burden. Cain has done what he believes is good and right, yet God doesn't regard the intent of his offering in the same way that he does Abel's. Further, because Cain hasn't tamed the sin that lurks at his door, he gives in to his disappointment and rejection, which he assumes is undeserved, and ultimately kills his brother in a jealous rage. Then in Genesis 4:9, after God asks a question of God's own ("Where is your brother Abel?"), we come to the grand question that Cain poses, the first big question in Scripture after Eden: "I do not know; *am I my brother's keeper?*"

AM I MY BROTHER'S KEEPER?

The philosopher Emmanuel Lévinas wrote about how the connection between human beings has been marred in modern society. In much of his early philosophical writing, which stemmed from the horror of the Holocaust during World War II, he pondered how it was possible that men and women could systematically seek to destroy an entire people group. To be human, Lévinas wrote, is to have a *face*, an identity that exudes the reality of God's image and likeness. Our *face* is seen when we gaze at each other and truly see the miracle of another living, breathing person, and they behold our *face* as well. The notion of *face* is so real and luminous that when we approach another human being the recognition of the divine in them should call forth in us the words "Thou shalt not kill" (Ex 20:13 KJV). This can only truly happen when we draw near enough to truly see with intimacy who we are standing before—what is referred to in the French as face-to-face (*rapport de face à face*) in deep nearness (*proximité*). In the depths of our soul, we are to acknowledge others' humanity and therefore accept our responsibility to protect them, nurture them, and seek to care for them.[9]

Those ideas are similar to what Augustine of Hippo said about our humanity in the fourth century. Our tie to the image of God, he wrote, is so deep within us that the *imago Dei* cannot be destroyed: it is bound to every fiber of our being. To see another human then is to see the evidence of the Creator within them.[10] Yet humans still do harm to other humans, as evidenced by the horrors that continue to plague our streets and the world. For St. Augustine as well as Lévinas, humans can commit harm and even murder because they can choose to disregard God, seeing only the creatureliness of the other person rather than evidence of their Creator. To forget that I, along with every other human being, am made in the image and likeness of God is to allow for the safety protocols of our ethics to be lifted and the nuclear weapons of destruction to be armed and deployed.

Some years ago I was traveling home from a conference and got stuck at O'Hare Airport in Chicago. Normally I am fairly casual with life in an airport, but not that time: it was my birthday, my wife had planned a party with a number of longtime friends, and I was excited to get home and celebrate. But by the time my second flight was canceled, I was starting to get a bit, well, agitated, and in a scene reminiscent of *Planes, Trains & Automobiles* where Steve Martin's character loses his cool with a ticketing agent, I began to raise my voice very loudly for all to hear at the ticketing counter, as though that would solve my woes.

At that time, I was an associate pastor of a small church, and in the midst of my rant at the counter, someone in line behind me tapped my shoulder. I turned around, still red faced from yelling at the poor airline employee, and looked into the eyes of a woman who happened to be an elder in the church I was serving as a pastor.

Suffice it to say that I was instantly ashamed of my behavior, knowing full well that whatever sense of pastoral decorum I might have had before that moment had surely washed away. To use Lévinas's term, the woman from my church had seen my *face*. She had seen with incredible clarity the brokenness of who I really was. In a large airport, hundreds of miles from my home, I had somehow forgotten myself and my *face* in the world. I had absentmindedly slipped into anonymity for myself and others, and as a result I hadn't taken into account the image of God in the *face* of the ticketing agent.

In my impatience and desire to get home, I had allowed my disappointment to get the best of me, and I took it out on someone else, as though it wouldn't have consequences. But in a split second, all it took was for me to be seen, for my *face* to be acknowledged by someone I knew from another context, and I was snapped back into who I was and the responsibility I had for others as people created by the living God. After apologizing to the ticketing agent for my behavior and heading off to my departure gate, I was again left alone to consider who I was and my responsibility for other people and how I treat people even if they are strangers.

This is what Cain is questioning God about with his pointed query in Genesis 4:9. "Am I my brother's keeper?" is a bold question that in some ways is simply rhetorical for Cain. He doesn't seem to want an answer, preferring instead to try to plant an ethical flag through his actions. Cain's question basically asks, "To what extent am I connected to other people?" Or to use Jesus' imagery from John 15, at what point is a branch somehow unique, individual from the vine? In our work with refugee resettlement it is difficult to get some people to move beyond the political and economic reality that comes with "refugee" unless there is a time and a place to have some basic common life together. Especially in a polarized age when people retreat into their various echo-chamber tribes, when people demonize the other and seem to be lacking in general empathy for people in different circumstances, the level where I see myself intimately connected to other people who are not like me becomes vitally important.

As Jesus makes abundantly clear in John 15, to be alive is to be connected and grafted into others (branches) and to the source of life itself (the vine). To be individual, to live as though we're not responsible for others, is the path of withering, ultimately leading to death. As we saw in Genesis 1–3, were we never meant to be alone, and now in Genesis 4 we are reminded that to be alive is to care, nurture, protect, sustain, seek justice, and have mercy and grace for others.

Both of the questions we have looked at thus far—"Where are you?" (Gen 3:9) and "Am I my brother's keeper?" (Gen 4:9)—revolve around the intimacy and care that are only found in relationships. They draw vertical and horizontal spiritual location points, pointing upward in relation to God and outward in relation to others. How we ask both questions will provide a good indicator of the state of our body, our mind, and our soul, and might give a clue as to what sort of things afflict and tempt us, what might be lurking at the door of our soul. Imagine a world where the answers to "Where are you?" and "Am I my brother's keeper?" could be answered with the connectedness of John 15 and the intimacy of a branch connected to the vine.

What would our society look like if we truly embraced our responsibility to be our brothers' and sisters' keepers? What if by acknowledging our deep responsibility and care for others, we could live in communities of care and compassion rather than in isolation, fear, mistrust, and violence?

Cain separates himself from being "known" (*yada*), thereby also severing his connection with his brother, with his family, and with the God who created and sustained him. His implied "no" to his own powerful question, as seen through his murder of Abel, leaves him withering as a dying branch on the vine of life.

Even this, however, isn't the end for Cain, nor is it the end of humanity's capacity to be connected to God and others. As we saw in the first verses of Genesis 4, our lives as *known* people are marked deeply by God's creative action. We are all image bearers of the Creator, a fact that isn't destroyed even when we allow the sin lurking at our doorway to come in and seize us. While even in the twenty-first century the name of Cain still carries an image of murder and disobedience, it isn't the full story, because God's mercy still gets the final word: "Then the Lord said to him, 'Not so! Whoever kills Cain will suffer a sevenfold vengeance.' And the Lord put a mark on Cain, so that no one who came upon him would kill him" (Gen 4:15).

THE MARK OF CAIN AND THE MARK OF BLESSING

In the reception of this passage throughout the centuries, many teachers of the Bible have scratched their heads over the idea of the "mark of Cain." Is it a mark of condemnation and public humiliation, like the shaming of Hester Prynne with a red *A* in *The Scarlet Letter*?[11] Or might it be something more supernatural, like the lightning-bolt scar across Harry Potter's forehead, marking him as "the boy who lived"?[12] Whatever form Cain's mark takes, it ensures that everyone he encounters will know he has been touched and preserved for life by the living God. Throughout Scripture, the notion of *blessing* is similar to the idea of Cain's mark. To be blessed is to be marked, which can amount to a burden to bear in the world. The burden of blessing is that God's love has reached out in spite of who we are, where we live, who we surround ourselves with, and whatever actions we may do to separate ourselves from the living vine of God's power. To bear the burden of blessing means that we will live with all that we are, all that we have been, and all that we will become, and that we will always have a witness—that we won't live this life alone. To bear the burden of blessing means that our *face* and the faces of others— unique, unrepeatable miracles of the living God that they are— will no longer be veiled or hidden.

We can no longer answer the question "Am I my brother's keeper?" in the negative. The burden of blessing is an assurance that the sin lurking at our doorway will not overcome all that God has in store for us. In short, Cain has become a witness to the power of God to save, to protect, and to sustain. When his name could have been tied only to death and isolation, under the burden of God's blessing he is instead marked as truly "the boy who lived," someone who will continue to live in the mercy and grace of the Creator and Sustainer of all things despite what he has done. It's a plot twist in the narrative, to be sure, but the longer we spend time with the living God, the more we will find that strange is the new normal. There is nothing predictable or pedestrian about the burden-bearing love of God.

"The God of the Bible is the strangest thing about the whole Bible," writes Walter Brueggemann, summing up his lifetime of Old Testament scholarship.

> In all the history of religion, there is no other like the God of the Bible. . . . So the people who dwelt with God in the Bible always want to relate to (God) like they relate to all other notions of God. And in every time, even ours today, we are tempted to force God into other categories as though God belongs to a species of similar agents. But God is not like any other. And God's strangeness is in this . . . God is with His people. God is for His people. God's goodness is not in the great transcendental power nor in the majestic remoteness nor in the demanding toughness but in the readiness to be with and for people. And being with and for is not a matter of bribery or deception or intimidation. God simply wills it so.[13]

Brueggemann's idea that "God is with His people," "God is for His people" is something we all need to hear again and again. The testimony of God's sustaining work with Cain in Genesis 4 is a reminder. Another illustration that adds potency to the promise that God is with the people and for all people is found in the film *Blood Diamond*. Based on true events, the film chronicles the burden of blessing, as a boy soldier comes to a point of "remembering" himself as a son and not as a killer.

Set in late-1990s Sierra Leone, the movie tells the story of Salomon Vandy, a fisherman who dreams of the day when his young son Dia will become a doctor, but whose dreams are shattered when rebels invade his village. Kidnapped to work in the diamond mines, and forcibly separated from Dia, Solomon happens upon an enormous pink diamond and tries to hide it. The commandant of the rebels sees it happen, but at that exact moment, the rebels running the mine are attacked and Solomon is arrested by the government army.

In the jail, the wounded commandant tells the other prisoners that Solomon has found the stone, prompting a mercenary smuggler named Danny Archer to release Solomon and propose exchanging the diamond for finding Solomon's missing family. Enlisting the help of an idealistic American journalist named Maddy Bowen, Archer locates Solomon's wife and daughters in a refugee camp but is informed that little Dia has been recruited by the rebels.

From then on, Solomon and Danny consolidate a partnership, Solomon searching for his son, Danny looking for a form of redemption in the midst of his own tragedies. Toward the end of the film, Solomon finally locates his son, who by this time has been forced into unspeakable acts of violence so atrocious that he thinks he is beyond saving. In a powerful moment of reconciliation, Solomon confronts his son and pleads with him to remember his true identity:

> Dia! What are you doing? Dia! . . . Look at me, look at me. What are you doing? You are Dia Vandy, of the proud Mende tribe. You are a good boy. You love soccer and school. Your mother loves you so much. She waits by the fire making plantains, and red palm oil stew with your sister and the new baby. The cows wait for you. And Babu, the wild dog who minds no one but you. I know they made you do bad things, but you are not a bad boy. I am your father who loves you. And you will come home with me and be my son again.[14]

As you reflect on the question of Cain and what it means to be bound to others in responsibility, think about ways that your own life has been shaped by those who have taken responsibility for knowing you. As we see in Solomon Vandy's powerful reminder to his son Dia, we are bound up in the lives of others in deep and abiding ways. We can forget who and what we are called to be if we forget these relationships. John 15 reminds us that as with a vine and its branches it is hard to know the beginning and end of the intimacy of connection we have to one another, yet once we are cut off from each other and the source of our life, the reality of our connection is seen and felt immediately.

To ask, "Am I my brother's/sister's keeper?" is to ask, "Am I truly in relationship and seeing my responsibility extending beyond merely caring for my needs and wants?" The good news is that we are never so far away that we can't grasp the hand of another who wants to love us back into what it means to be healed and whole again. The promise of the gospel extends beyond our capacity to run and hide. As Solomon Vandy says so well, God continues to reach out to us with the promise, "I am your father who loves you. And you will come home with me."

Take time in reflecting on the journey of Cain to consider how you find responsibility and relationship with others in your life right now and what "coming home" might mean. Is there a brother, sister, or other family member you are feeling estranged from and you feel the need to make amends? Is there a marginalized student or group on your campus that you can reach out to and build some understanding with? Is there some past hurt or loss you haven't shared with another person that you might now be ready to share and seek some help with reconciling? Are there groups or individuals you might have prejudices toward, yet you have never sat down and shared a cup of coffee or a meal with that you might be drawn to now in a sense of hospitality and discovery?

Be open to where the Spirit might lead you as you ask, "Am I my brother's keeper?" You may discover your connection and common humanity with others God draws you to.

3

HOW WILL I KNOW?

Questioning in Times of Uncertainty

God is not nice
God is not Uncle
God is an earthquake.

GILLIAN ROSE
"THE FINAL NOTEBOOKS"

Add to this that he was partly a young man of our time—
that is, honest by nature, demanding the truth, seeking it
and believing in it, and in that belief demanding immediate
participation in it with all the strength of his soul.

FEODOR DOSTOYEVSKY
THE BROTHERS KARAMAZOV

I s there a God? Where is God?" Those were the questions
someone recently asked in a moment of intense honesty, as he
told a story. "It is a really good question," he continued. "The
other day I was praying over something as I was running, and I
ended up saying to God, 'Look, this is all very well, but isn't it
about time you did something, if you're there?'"

Here's what was unusual about that particular moment: the person asking the question was the Archbishop of Canterbury, one of the highest-ranking officials of the Church of England. After his questionings made their way into a *New York Times* op-ed, the internet exploded as people all over the world reacted to the idea of a person in such a high position of leadership publicly questioning God's existence. Julia Baird, who wrote the op-ed, says that doubt has been a part of the Christian story for a long time. "Certainty is so often overrated," writes Baird. "This is especially the case when it comes to faith, or other imponderables." As she says later in the article, it's not that it's a problem to doubt; it's what we do with our doubts once we have them that becomes most important.[1]

If human beings were to resemble punctuation, we would probably be question marks. Imagine walking down the street and seeing a peacock of question marks hovering over each head. Imagine a trail of question marks hanging like a wedding train behind each person, floating on the breeze as they walk, leaving question mark–shaped particles of dust flittering down onto the sidewalk, coming to rest in the gutter as each of us continues to walk and ponder. That's the kind of image that arises for the writer of Psalm 8. See if you can spot the big question that the psalmist is asking.

O Lord, our Sovereign,
   how majestic is your name in all the earth!
You have set your glory above the heavens.
   Out of the mouths of babes and infants
you have founded a bulwark because of your foes,
   to silence the enemy and the avenger.

When I look at your heavens, the work of your fingers,
    the moon and the stars that you have established;
what are human beings that you are mindful of them,
    mortals that you care for them?

Yet you have made them a little lower than God,
    and crowned them with glory and honor.
You have given them dominion over the works of your
        hands;
    you have put all things under their feet,
all sheep and oxen,
    and also the beasts of the field,
the birds of the air, and the fish of the sea,
    whatever passes along the paths of the seas.

O LORD, our Sovereign,
    how majestic is your name in all the earth! (Ps 8)

In this magnificent poem, the psalmist goes from the very heights of heaven to the very depths of the sea, reveling in how the expansive creation testifies to the truth of God, how it screams that God is to be glorified. Yet in verse 4, there's a question mark: *What about human beings? What are humans, anyway?*

As human beings, we are the embodiment of questions. We ask them all the time, seeking, searching, exploring, plunging to the depths of things because we want to know more—we want to understand, to probe, to dig deeper. The psalmist finds that to be human means not only to ask questions but essentially to *be* a question, one that's directed to God. We question things. All of creation lays forth God's glory, but humans stand back and think; we pause to ponder what we see. The psalmist wonders, *Who are we?* And we wonder, *Who is God?*

Part of the journey of life is coming to grips with our identity as question askers and learning to see and hear our questions as strengths, not weaknesses. What are the good questions we should be asking, and how has Scripture equipped us to ask good questions of each other and of God?

This chapter moves the conversation forward as we look at the question of certainty and faith itself. What are we trusting when we say we have faith? How do we know that God is going to show up? Where is our certainty? When will doubt be filled with faith enough for us to move forward?

ABRAM, THE FATHER OF FAITH

In Genesis 12, we're introduced to Abram, a seventy-five-year-old man who is married to Sarai, age sixty-five. As the curtain opens, we find them having a pretty good life. They're living in the land of Abram's fathers, and they're materially comfortable. Then, out of the blue, the God of the universe shows up and calls to Abram, asking him to go to a land that Abram has never seen.

The crazy thing is, Abram follows! Imagine something like this happening to you. You're walking to class, waiting in line for coffee, or driving your car to work, and God says, "Go to the land I have for you." Rather than shake it off, Abram takes his wife, his nephew, and his livestock, and they go—they follow without a word.

Now, the Scripture could have simply lowered the curtain at this point, rolled the credits, and called it good; it's a pretty nice story. But it doesn't go that way. Abram is a human—and humans ask questions.

So as the story moves forward, Abram and his family make their way to Egypt, and Abram becomes worried about what might happen to Sarai. Finding himself as a stranger in a strange land, Abram moves away from faith and into fear. As with Adam and Eve in the garden, one of the first temptations that arises when we have fear is to mistrust others. He lies about his relationship with her, saying that she's his sister, not his wife, offering her up to the people that they meet out of fear for what might happen to his own safety if they find out that she's his wife.

When the Egyptians find out what's happened, they send Abram out of the country with Sarai, and the couple is on the run again. They roam around for a while, still trying to figure out what God had in mind by moving them. Finally, in Genesis 13, God comes to Abram again, telling them not to worry, because "I will make your offspring like the dust of the earth" (v. 16). "Abram," says God, "I've got a plan for you. I know it's taking a long time, but it's going to happen. It's going to work out. It's going to be fine."

Eventually Abram finds that he has enough faith to pick up and move on as God asks him to. Then, in chapter fifteen, God addresses Abram in a powerful way that will prove to be a game changer: "Do not be afraid, Abram, I am your shield; your reward shall be very great" (Gen 15:1). The three most important words here are *afraid*, *shield*, and *reward*, and they begin with a simple admonition: *don't* be afraid.

"DON'T BE AFRAID" IS
THE CANNON SHOT OF GOD

My family and I lived in Scotland for a time. In Edinburgh, the medieval city, there is a castle sitting on a dormant volcano next to a large mound called Arthur's Seat, right in the middle of town. Edinburgh Castle is grand, beautiful, and almost imposingly gorgeous. At one o'clock in the afternoon most days, the city suddenly reverberates with the sound of an explosion as the cannons atop the walls at Edinburgh Castle are fired. It's a longstanding tradition in Edinburgh, and the reason traces back to preindustrial days as a means of warning ships as they were coming into the Port of Leith two miles away. The eastern coast of Scotland is often foggy, so dense that the Scots even have a term for it: the *haar*. It rolls in and covers everything, obscuring the land and making it impossible for ship crews to see the coastline. As a result, sailors of long ago wouldn't be able to tell what time it was or how close they were to Edinburgh, covered over in the *haar* as their ships were, so the cannon at Edinburgh Castle would be fired at exactly one o'clock every day to give the fog-blinded seafarers an exact indicator of what time it was and where the shore was located. As a captain in the Port of Leith, you might have thought that it was such-and-such a time, you may have thought you were located in such-and-such a place, and you may have been correct or wildly wrong, with no way of knowing. But once you heard the cannon shot, you knew exactly what time it was and exactly where you were.

What God is doing with Abram in Genesis is firing a cannon shot through the *haar* of the world to shake him out of the aimlessness and fog of his life, to reset his clock and his compass in relation to God's designs. "Do not be afraid" is the cannon shot of God. It's an explosion we hear over and over again in the Scriptures: in the early history of God's people through Abram's life, down through the prophets, and all the way through the Annunciation to Mary: do not be afraid, the Lord your God is with you. Just as the sound reverberates through Edinburgh in the afternoon, the invitation of "Do not be afraid" reverberates through time to us today in our own lives and contexts, wherever we find ourselves.

God's promise to Abram comes in two more pieces as well. God also promises to be a "shield" for him (Gen 15:1). The word *shield* in Hebrew also refers to the great scales on the leviathans, sea creatures of the deep. In other words, the shield that is being promised to Abram is not a dinky little shield that can protect against the ping-ping-ping of little arrows. This is a big shield, huge, like the size of leviathan in the depths of the sea. It is so massive, so enormous, that it will surround you and protect you from anything you can imagine or haven't even thought of yet. It's an expansive shield, one that God promises will protect on land and in the darkest corners of the ocean.

Last, God's promise involves "reward" (Gen 15:1). The Hebrew word here, *sakar*, has to do with wages for people who work. But it also has another resonance. Certain words in Hebrew are like tuning forks, in the sense that they have something like an overtone, perhaps sounding like something else as a way of hinting toward a deeper meaning. Another word that is used in later chapters is the word *salaq*, which means "to set afire" and would have sounded to the Hebrews similar to the word *sakar*. What it means is that the reward Abram will get is not just wages but something lit, something bright and burning and warm that will cast away darkness. This is a burning reward, something that's going to be out there chasing darkness from the roads and from the ways and from the byways. It will be something to challenge the idols of the age and any other dark, scary, or fear-inducing things that are coming Abram's way.

So, "Do not be *afraid*" . . . I am your *shield*; your *reward* shall be very great." This promise of God is the context for the first part of what Abram hears. Abram comes from a land and a people that are distracted by the many gods of their cultures. As much as God is telling Abram who he is as the one true God, Abram now hears that he can fall into the tradition that he comes from if he's not careful, sliding back into the practices of idol worship like those from the land that he came from.

In Neil Gaiman's novel *American Gods*, a newly released convict named Shadow discovers that the world in America is a bit different from what he had thought. As he drives from place to place, he finds that the streets and alleys of America are filled with little gods that people have been creating, and these gods run to and fro demanding worship from the humans around them. "People believe," says Shadow.

> It's what people do. They believe, and then they do not take responsibility for their beliefs; they conjure things. . . . People populate the darkness; with ghosts, with gods, with electrons, with tales. People imagine, and people believe; and it is that rock solid belief, that makes things happen.[2]

Earlier in the book another character also comments,

> There are new gods growing in America, clinging to growing knots of belief: gods of credit card and freeway, of Internet and telephone, of radio and hospital and television, gods of plastic

and of beeper and of neon. Proud gods, fat and foolish creatures, puffed up with their own newness and importance.[3]

What Gaiman proposes in the book has application to our life
of faith. In the story, Americans are so taken up with creating
their own little gods that they give them everything that they
are, their energy, their attention, their fixation, and their love.
But when we empty ourselves of praise onto these so-called
gods, fear will take root.

FEAR IS FED BY WORSHIPING
THE WRONG THINGS IN LIFE

In Genesis 15:1, God tells Abram to break his culture's habit of
paying attention to the little gods and to pay attention instead
to the One who is going to take him into his promise. As Abram
hears this promise, he is also reminded that he's heard it before.
"O Lord God," he replies, "what will you give me, for I continue
childless, and the heir of my house is Eliezer of Damascus?"
Abram continues, "You have given me no offspring, and so a
slave born in my house is to be my heir" (Gen 15:2-3). Abram
is essentially responding to God's promise with protest, just like
we often do in our own lives. When we are drawn into a relationship of promise, and we feel that it might be too big, too
overwhelming, or too impossible for us to imagine, often our
first port of call is protest.

That's what Abram is doing here because God's promise to
Abram calls out Abram's biggest fear from somewhere deep
inside him. When God makes a promise to us, it often has the
unexpected effect of calling out the thing we most fear in order
to show us where our worship and praise is focused. Abram's

greatest fear is that he'll have no heir, that he'll have to adopt a slave to keep his family's legacy moving forward. He'll have to take a shortcut to get to what God wants to do. He can be given all the land in Canaan, all the milk and honey he wants, but without an heir, it all seems pointless. Without a child, he has nothing, and he knows that he's not getting any younger. God's powerful promise comes boldly forward, right into Abram's ear, and Abram immediately begins pushing with powerful resistance and protest to keep it at a distance.

Abram's example calls us to think about how we would respond too. When God is inviting you into a deeper and more trustworthy relationship, what arises in you as a reason to resist?

Perhaps you're hearing God call you to change your course of study or your job; there's something about your career path at present, and you know maybe you've come to the end and need to do something different. What arises in you as a reason not to take the leap and change course? Where is that coming from?

Or maybe you're feeling the pull to downsize your lifestyle, like you're buried under debt and you're trying to juggle too many parts of your lifestyle in the air, spinning too many plates, going crazy just to satisfy your creditors without going hungry, and you'd love to downsize and get simpler. What's stopping you from doing that? What's fearful in that move?

Maybe you have a vision for your family, the types of people and friends you need to be around, the support network you need to have, and you need to make a change in order for that to happen. Or maybe you need to confront somebody you have a broken relationship with; you need to be the one to make the first move to reconcile. What is the resistance in that? What's stopping you?

The point is, when God is inviting you into a place where God can identify your fear to you, what's the resistance in facing and dealing with what God shows you? When we feel our sense of protest arising to counter God's call, it actually shows us exactly where we need to lean into God's presence even more, not less—and why is it so difficult to lean into what God is showing us?

Twenty years ago, I was at a crossroads in my life. I was trying to decide about a job change along with some decisions about relationships, and I was stuck. I didn't have the answers in my own head, and I prayed about it, but I was feeling a sense of God's silence about it all. So I wrote letters to fourteen people I knew—some I knew really well and others I just trusted for counsel and authority in my life. That probably sounds pretty Victorian, but I literally wrote letters, licked envelopes, put stamps on them, and dropped them in the mailbox. Mailing the letters was my way of saying, "I need your discernment. I need your insight into my life. Speak into my life. I'm giving you permission to do that."

I had a grand plan: I was going to get all of these letters back, bundle them up, drive away, and over the course of two weeks, open a letter each morning and another one at night, allowing the wisdom and insight to guide my days. It was going to be a grand journey of discovery.

In those days I was driving a 1986 Jeep CJ-7, which was already beaten up and old at this point, and I loaded my letters into the back seat along with my sleeping bag and tent with the goal of driving to Arches National Park in Utah. I was going to have a desert experience, and it would be awesome. With resolve and focus, I headed out from my home in Seattle, ultimately bound for the deserts of the Beehive State.

When you ask people for input, they usually give you input. Every single person sent a letter back to me, so before I left, I was holding the letters in a bundle and thought, *Okay, now what's in the envelopes?* I knew even then that they held something I needed to hear.

Driving through southern Idaho in July, it got very hot. My Jeep CJ-7 was a gas guzzler, and a Jeep isn't necessarily the safest automobile. This one had the windscreen in front, and the only way they could put a rearview mirror on was to glue the mirror onto the glass. Somewhere around Twin Falls, Idaho, the mirror literally melted off and fell into my lap. From that moment, I was driving without a rearview mirror, and I spent the next fifty miles or so trying to hold it up with one hand while steering with the other.

The car ended up overheating, and I was stuck in Idaho with what turned out to be a $1,000 repair needed to get the Jeep going again.

My plans were shot to oblivion, and I was stranded. I'd had this picture of where God was going to take me, and I was going to have my discernment period and experience nirvana in the desert. I was going to get to Utah and open those letters, and it was going to be amazing: I would know *exactly* what God wanted from my life. Instead, on my way to Utah, I was $1,000 in debt with no way to pay for it. So I had to call people to get some help. "Hey," I'd say to a friend or a family member over the payphone, "can you spot me some money so I can get out of here and get on to where I'm supposed to go?"

But I still had those letters, and even while I was stuck, I made time to read them. As I opened them over the course of a few days, I was finally dislodged from the doldrums of self-pity and brought out into the fresh air of God's discernment. I needed to change jobs, it became clear to me. I needed to make some moves in my life toward closer, more accountable relationships. I needed to get more serious about my spiritual life. I needed to take better care of myself.

Over and over these letters called me to task, as voice after gentle voice came up from the handwriting and pushed me deeper into the heartbeat of God. I wasn't on the journey I had thought I would be, and I wasn't having the desert spiritual retreat that I thought I needed. Yet, somehow, in this space of unexpected car malfunctions and financial freefall, the humility that God wanted to give me opened me up to see and hear him anew.

Once I finally returned to Seattle, I found that what I had thought were the questions I needed to ask weren't the right ones. I didn't look for a new job—I applied to graduate school and eventually moved to Scotland. I took the leap and got the courage to ask my girlfriend (now wife of over twenty years) to marry me. And I sold the Jeep because I found that the question wasn't how to keep the Jeep running but how to make my life more financially responsible, and having a money pit with four-wheel drive was not what I needed. Once I was asked different questions by those I trusted for discernment, my life radically changed in ways I never expected, and it is better for those different questions.

What's happening to Abram in Genesis 15 is similar to my unexpected misadventure on I-84 somewhere near the Utah state line. Abram is in a place where he wants God to show up in the way *Abram* wants God to show up. He wants God to do things according to Abram's plan and Abram's urgency, and it's not working out that way. But God is still showing up.

The name *Israel*—the descendants of the people who later came from Abram—literally means, "the ones who have wrestled with God." It's the name change Jacob received when he wrestled a divine visitor in Genesis 32. This legacy of Israel, struggling with God and wrestling with God and asking big questions of God, has been part of the program of faith. It's never been true that we sign up for a relationship with God, and we get a nice certificate of participation just for showing up. It is a wrestling match, a struggle, like Jacob in his wrestling, Abram in his doubts, and thirtysomething Jeff stranded on the roadside on exactly the kind of desert retreat he didn't ask for. It's in those moments of wrestling, of unknowns, of felt dependency on God's care that we finally get in the right posture to listen. In those moments we ask big questions, protests and all; God even lets us protest because it gets us to show how we really feel toward God. We come clean with our fears, our brokenness, and our disappointment, becoming more real, more *raw* with a God who wants to know us, warts and all.

Scripture is filled with examples of individuals digging deep and getting real with God: Esther resisting the call to action, Job crying aloud to the Lord while sitting on the ash heap of his former life, Paul debating the Athenians, wrestling and struggling with ideas and doubts and wondering out loud. Visceral questions have always been part of this story. Abram has put the promises before him, and he's wrestling with them.

Aaron Zeitlin, a past professor of Hebrew literature at the Jewish Theological Seminary in New York, was a wonderful writer of poetry and of novels. In his poem "If You Look at the Stars" Zeitlin describes the reality of wrestling with and challenging God. In the short poem written from God to the reader, God pleads with us to sing his praises and cry out in our anguish and frustration because in the end, says God, "If you don't praise and you don't revile / Then I created you in vain."

We need to be honest with God if we expect to have a deeper relationship with the One who created and loves us. Part of that might involve protest, opening up our hearts and allowing our biggest fears to be shown: "God, you're not showing up fast enough. God, it's not turning out how I wanted it to be." This is exemplified in Abram's question as protest before God. But God still listens, still gets close, and isn't ashamed of Abram's wonderings.

God's response is peculiar and odd and awesome all at once. "Look toward heaven," God says to Abram after taking him outside, "and count the stars, if you are able to count them. . . . So shall your descendants be" (Gen 15:5). Think about that for a moment. The context in which Abram is asking all these questions is in a tent, a tent of his making, a tent that he's putting up, constructing. It has a nice, taught line hitch to make sure the stake is in properly, probably a ridgepole going across, nice flaps—a decent tent. That's where Abram is located, but God wants him to get outside his tent to get a bigger picture. We ask God questions in the context of what we can control, and we want God to show up in the place we control because then it works on our behalf and to our advantage. But that's not how the God of the universe works.

LOOKING THROUGH THE WRONG
SIDE OF THE BINOCULARS

When I was nine years old, I was taking a ferry to my grand-father's cabin. During the crossing, I borrowed my uncle's bin-oculars to look at the shoreline that was coming, but I couldn't see anything. My uncle took the binoculars, flipped them, handed them back, and said, "You're looking through the wrong side. You have to look through this side." I put them up, and boom! Everything was close and big.

Abram is looking through the wrong end of his binoculars in Genesis 15. He's in his closed, cloistered tent, and he can only see as far as the ceiling. But God invites him out, throwing the flap doors open, and shows him the grandeur of the universe. In the midst of all of this, he essentially says, "I am the Lord God, the one who's providing for you, caring for you, hoping for you, and I am going to do this for you." He shakes Abram out of his sleeping bag, gets him stargazing, and says, "Let's look at the bigger picture here. Let's look at the context in which I am."

Evidently it was just what Abram needed. Abram "believed the Lord; and the Lord reckoned it to him as righteousness" (Gen 15:6). As human beings, we are perpetually swinging back and forth into fear and out again. Fear is such a part of our lives that it's hard to even notice it, like fish swimming upstream. We're so used to pushing against it, swimming through it, that we may not even realize it's moving us away from the place we want to go. Our fears and anxieties populate our lives in big and small ways, which is Abram's experience in his wanderings. But God calls Abram out on his biggest fear, wanting to know and be known by Abram in spite of his fear. No longer can Abram fit his life inside this tent. It won't work. Once God gets him outside and focusing on God's bigness instead of Abram's smallness, Abram binds his life to God, not to a plan, not to a program but to the person of God. And in that binding, in that covenant relationship being established, God will take him to the place Abram needs to go.

Even under the stars, Abram still wants to know. "O Lord God, how am I to know that I shall possess it?" (Gen 15:8). How am I to know that I'm going to fulfill this? How am I to know that this is going to happen? Abram's relationship with God has been solidified—and even though he is now a man of faith, he is still willing to risk asking God the questions that are on his heart, only this time, it's from a standpoint of confidence in God's ability to deliver.

As the Archbishop of Canterbury reminded us at the beginning of this chapter, doubts are part of faith.[4] They're part of our story. They remind us of the loose soil that we're on, and they push us back into the grace of God. Here God chooses not to give Abram a plan or a program but to give Abram God's own self in the form of what we call a covenant. We set up contracts all the time in our lives as we do transactions with people: you sell me *that* and I'll give you *this*. That's not God's concern here; God is much more interested in the person. Who will Abram's children be when he becomes the father of nations? How will his journey make him the person who is going to fulfill God's promises to the world?

CHOOSING A GUIDE OVER A MAP

Earl Palmer, who was a pastor in Seattle, used to say that we hunger after a map for our lives. We just want some kind of easy-to-read schematic, some Marauder's Map like you'd find at Hogwarts ("mischief managed!") so that we can know where we are and what we're doing.[5] *If I can just get a map*, we think, *that's all I need.* But God doesn't give us maps. He gives us himself as a guide because that's what we really need: a guide. Any map is limited; it only shows so much. But God is going to take you off-road. He's going to take you to places you would never suspect or even dream of, and you need God *himself* to take you there.

Abram's story is going to take another twenty-five years before he gets to have his promised son, called Isaac, this son of laughter. Besides that, God's promises to Abram are going to fall on his descendants, not on Abram himself, such that Abram won't even get to see the fulfillment of all the visions that God has given him. He's not going to see his descendants, like stars in the night sky, populating the world. God's promises are larger than Abram himself, and Abram is going to be a part of the story, but he has to realize that his faith is for his chapter, not for everything.

When I was in Scotland, I worked as an assistant minister at the Glasgow Cathedral for a time. Glasgow has an odd origin story. It was founded by a monk, St. Kentigern, from the Isle of Iona, who was feeling called by God to come to this land and to share the gospel. He took a boat, came to the shore, and met a man with an oxcart, and said to him (I'm paraphrasing), "God has told me to go with you and find a place and to plant a church." The guy with the oxcart said, "Sure, all right," and he brought St. Kentigern into the oxcart to sit beside him.

Suddenly, the man who owned the oxcart died, leaving St. Kentigern with a corpse, an ox, and a confused look. "Well, okay, God," he said. "I guess you're going to show me where I'm to bury this man and consecrate that land, and that will be the place where I'm meant to go." So he asked the ox to lead him, and the ox led him to a pool of water.

The name for Glasgow comes from the Gaelic for "dear green place," and it's all because, according to the story, it was founded on the place where St. Kentigern found a clear pool to water his ox, bury the man, and begin building a community. He started with that simple thing, and from that, he had a vision of something that was going to be bigger than his life. People started to gather near that pool of water. They started to grow food and build buildings. Slowly but surely a little community started to rise up.

In time, the community was big enough to become a town, and a city, and the people built a cathedral along the way. This grand church that I served in took a couple hundred years to build and became the site of what was the beginning a grand city that has launched ships, created industries, and housed untold thousands of people over the centuries. So many things started from that one little act of mercy that was larger than St. Kentigern ever dreamed of seeing. His faithfulness in the moment was all that mattered.

God's promise to you is like that. God wants to take you somewhere that is larger than your life, more all-encompassing than your wildest dreams—and it's going to be for the generations to behold.

I really miss my Jeep that broke down. It was a great car. But I don't miss the debt. I never got to Utah on that trip, let alone to Arches National Park. But I was alone that time. A few years ago, however, I finally made it to Arches, along with my wife and three daughters. Standing in that place, surrounded by my family, I was basking in the fulfillment of God's provision that I never could have seen during that ill-fated adventure so many years ago. In that fulfillment, twenty years in the making, was everything that God had hoped for but I hadn't been ready for two decades prior. Granted, it was also twenty years that included more loss and suffering in other ways, so don't think that this is a Disney ending where everything wraps up with a song in our hearts that is only in major chords. Plenty of refrains in minor keys played over the years as well. But in the midst of it all, God brought me back to see and experience this in his time and through the right side of the binoculars.

And this is what God is saying to us. He has made a promise to push us onward, and it's not just for Abram, it's not just for me—it's for you. This promise is for *you*. And your protests and your fears? Listen to the cannon shot of God reminding you of where you are and what time it is. Do not be afraid, but tell God what your fears are so he can deal with them. Get them out there. Be bold. Even protest; God can take it. But know that the provision to fulfill God's promise is going to be found in the presence of God, if you and I will have the courage to wait with him and let him fulfill his incredible plans for us.

4

WHO AM I?

Questions of Shame, Fear, and Identity

*The fear from the past is not allowed
to thwart the redemptive promise of the future.*

BREVARD S. CHILDS
THE BOOK OF EXODUS

*This is my name forever,
and this my title for all generations.*

EXODUS 3:15

Some time ago, I was going for a run around Seattle's Green Lake Park, and I caught sight of a runner with a dog coming toward me. From my great distance, I was puzzled to see that the dog was wearing a strange collar. As they got closer, I could see that the runner was a serious one, very focused, and the dog was a Weimaraner, a gorgeous, purebred dog with a grayish tone in its fur, very majestic and sleek. The dog and the runner were moving just like pistons, really "in the zone," and they were coming toward me, which meant that I wanted to run like I really knew what I was doing.

As I got closer to the runner and the dog, I noticed that the Weimaraner's ears seemed extremely flappy, wagging around in all directions in the breeze. As I finally came to where I could see both the runner and his dog in detail, I noticed that the dog—this beautiful animal that stood atop the generations of careful breeding—was wearing two bags of what we'll call "dog dirt" tied to its collar. The owner had scooped up after the dog, tied the bags of dog dirt to its collar, and continued to run. Now, with every pace as the dog ran, it was being slapped on either side of its head by the stuff that had been scooped up. What I had thought were flappy ears and a weird collar were actually normal Weimaraner ears and a typical collar. What was flapping and bouncing with the rhythm of the run was a pair of receptacles of the dog's own dirt.

Frankly, it was one of the most absurd and shameful pictures I've ever seen, and rarely have I seen something so demoralizing. The dog didn't deserve the treatment it was getting. It was a magnificent dog, but it was being hit over and over, back and forth, on its own head by its own waste, as it was going along. I'm sure the runner thought it was an efficient way of doing things, but my mind instantly went to an analogy: it's just like some of the stories we write for ourselves. We live our lives bludgeoning ourselves with shame, tying it to ourselves, running through life with it strapped to us, deciding to become used to being hit over and over by our own shame and brokenness as if it's simply the way of the world. As people of faith, we sometimes learn to accept what is essentially absurd, going around the circles of our lives over and over again, trying to get a sense of meaning and purpose while always beating ourselves up with shame. We become so used to it that we even learn to rely on the rhythm our shame makes as it bounces against us, setting the rhythm of our very souls like the bounce, bounce, bounce of the doggie bags.

"The fear from the past," wrote Old Testament scholar Brevard Childs, "is not allowed to thwart the redemptive promise of the future."[1] I want you to hold onto that statement as we explore the life of Moses in Exodus 3 because Moses' story is one of shame, of carrying the burden of a life unfulfilled, of going through year after year of movement and journeying but seeming to go nowhere. As we'll see, Moses' fear of his own past has immobilized him, leading him to settle into a predictable and safe life, but one that wasn't going to cause very many problems for others or for himself. That fear of the past, in a sense, was his barricade against any possibility of change, of being all that he could be.

THE ORIGIN OF A HERO

The story of Moses is familiar to many of us, whether it's from the animated, singing Moses of *The Prince of Egypt* or the bewhiskered Charlton Heston version, arms raised with beard flapping in the wind in *The Ten Commandments* or Christian Bale's rendition from the movie *Exodus: Gods and Kings*. (It's interesting to think about Batman playing Moses, but I digress.) Regardless of the face you put on Moses, his story is pretty amazing. In Exodus 2 we hear one of the most famous hero-origin stories in history, which is mirrored in Superman's origin story with baby Kal-El's rocket from Krypton being sent to Earth. As a baby, Moses is placed in a basket to float down the Nile, where he is discovered and adopted by Pharaoh's daughter. Growing up in Pharaoh's household, he rises to power but always remains the nonbiological son in the family. He is in the household of power, standing in a place of privilege, but as he walks through his life he becomes enraged by the injustice that he sees. He identifies injustice in the street, ultimately seeing an Israelite being hit and beaten by an Egyptian. Moses kills the violent soldier and then flees the consequences of his deed. As we hear in Exodus 2:11, Moses meets his true people discovering that he is actually a Jew by birth, and not part of Pharaoh's biological family, which means that he is now split between worlds. *I don't fit into Pharaoh's household,* he thinks, *but I don't fully fit into the life of Israel either because I didn't feel the whip on my back. I don't have the story of the slave in my own background. Where do I fit?*

So here is Moses, at the age of forty, on the run, a fugitive. As Exodus 3 begins, Moses is an eighty-year-old man—four decades on the run, forty years of telling himself over and over that he didn't fit in Egypt and he didn't fit in his new home in self-imposed exile. He marries into a family and becomes a shepherd, working for his now father-in-law, Jethro, moving the livestock back and forth across the grazing lands. He settles into a calm, pastoral life, not causing any ripples. But in all of it he has also seemingly lost everything. His social capital is gone, he's a foreigner, he's broken, and shame continues to bludgeon him every day of his life. He has failed as a prince; he is mostly forgotten.

THE PAST IS PROLOGUE

At the start of Exodus 3, we encounter Moses leading his flock as he has so many times before. The form of the verbs here shows that he has done this task over and over again. Jethro's name is included in the chapter to reinforce that Moses is working his commitments: he's just doing his job, and nothing is going to change.

It's at that moment that things do change, but it's hard for us to imagine that, isn't it, stuck in our everyday ruts as we often are? How many times have we driven up and down a freeway, going to work? How many times have we listened to the same story on the same radio station, listened to the same song, ordered the same sandwich for lunch? In our heart of hearts, we often don't expect anything to change, and we assume every day will be the same. Granted, there are a number of "same old same old" things that I love: replaying classic albums over and over, coffee every morning, seeing my family at the end of a long day, the beginning of a new year on campus, and meeting a new generation of college freshmen each fall. But sometimes we can pave a deep rut through practices we do over and over that can blind us to something new and perhaps life changing.

SOMETIMES THE EXTRAORDINARY IS IN THE MIDST OF THE MUNDANE

In *Auggie Wren's Christmas Story*, Paul Auster tells the story of a time when he went into a Brooklyn cigar shop. As he walked in, the owner, a man by the name of Auggie Wren, offered to show Auster his great art project.

"God knows what I was expecting," Auster writes,

> At the very least, it wasn't what Auggie showed me the next day. In a small, windowless room at the back of the store, he opened a cardboard box and pulled out twelve identical black photo albums. This was his life's work, he said, and it didn't

take him more than five minutes a day to do it. Every morning for the past twelve years, he had stood on the corner of Atlantic Avenue and Clinton Street at precisely seven o'clock and had taken a single color photograph of precisely the same view.[2]

Auster begins sorting through the photographs and notes that the project ran for thousands of photographs, each album a different year, all different pictures, laid out in sequence from January 1 to December 31, all dated, all carefully curated in these beautiful albums.

> My first impression was that it was the oddest, most bewildering thing I had ever seen. All the pictures were the same. The whole project was a numbing onslaught of repetition, the same street and the same buildings over and over again, an unrelenting delirium of redundant images. I couldn't think of anything to say to Auggie, so I continued turning pages, nodding my head in feigned appreciation. Auggie himself seemed unperturbed, watching me with a broad smile on his face, but after I'd been at it for several minutes, he suddenly interrupted me and said, "You're going too fast. You'll never get it if you don't slow down."
>
> He was right, of course. If you don't take the time to look, you'll never manage to see anything. I picked up another album and forced myself to go more deliberately.[3]

Auster tells that as he started to look at each photograph next to another, he started to notice that different people would appear at different times, sometimes the same person wearing different clothes, sometimes a different stance. Sometimes their faces were sad, but sometimes he could see that their faces were changed, that they were having a bad day already. The subtle changes over time could only be experienced when he slowed down to look at the same thing closely enough to see that maybe something else was going on.[4] Social media is a place where people have drawn our attention to the easily overlooked as well. Facebook compiles posting retrospectives each year so you can see the trends you might have missed. A guy on Instagram recently took a series of pictures of himself with a sign asking his girlfriend to marry him with the girlfriend in the background of all the pictures not seeing what he was doing. You never know what extraordinary thing might be happening right under your nose if you don't take a moment to look intentionally at everything around you, including that which you have looked at for weeks, months, or years, but perhaps with new eyes and an open heart.

Moses, in his repetition and rote activity of "same old same old," was taking each moment of his life too fast as well. In many ways, Moses, as we see in Exodus 3:1, is just trying to get done with life. *Can I just finish out now?* he might be wondering to himself as he crosses the land with the livestock one more time. *Because nothing's going to change; this is what my lot is, and I'm just going to keep going.* But it's in the midst of this repetition and lack of attentiveness that God often shows up. In verse 2, Moses looks and sees: "There the angel of the LORD appeared to him in a flame of fire out of a bush; he looked, and the bush was blazing, yet it was not consumed."

How many times do we experience this part of Moses' story for ourselves? How many bushes and trees do we pass by without stopping to see if maybe they're ablaze? How many times do we drive so fast through the city that we cannot see the pain and suffering on a person's face as we pass by? How many times have we run for exercise and gone so fast—in our own zone, tuned into our own music—that we don't allow the Holy Spirit to open our mind to think, *What's on that person's mind? Maybe I should pray for her right now?* What we see happening in Exodus 3 is a grand interruption in Moses' life, a break in the monotony of his exiled existence. It's a reminder to us that we need our monotony broken as well.

"We must be ready to allow ourselves to be interrupted by God," wrote Dietrich Bonhoeffer in *Life Together.* "God will be constantly crossing our paths and canceling our plans by sending us people with claims and petitions."[5] This is what is going on with Moses, and it brings us to another point worth considering: God is in the business not only of bringing us into his heart; he's also giving us a people to be with, a community we get to work out his plan with. The astonishing thing that occurs in Moses' journey with God at this point is that God wants to bring him to a people—the people of Israel—*now,* fully and completely. We see in this divine encounter that God is not alone, and Moses is not alone with him. Moses shows up on the mountaintop expecting to be isolated with his livestock, having his own alone time, but we actually see that God is with him, calling him into a place and a people.

WHEN WHERE YOU ARE BECOMES WHO YOU ARE

This new place now binds Moses in his identity to God and to the people of Israel, who he is being called to. It's a huge move on God's part, and Moses hides his face from the identity of God, not believing that he can be bound to God anymore. He's been hungering after some kind of purpose in his life for so long that he's forgotten who he is. But then the Lord speaks.

"I have observed the misery of my people who are in Egypt," the Lord says to Moses. "I have heard their cry on account of their taskmasters. Indeed, I know their sufferings, and I have come down to deliver them from the Egyptians, and to bring them up out of that land to a good and broad land, a land flowing with milk and honey" (Ex 3:7-8). In that moment of the burning bush, God essentially burns away Moses' isolation. Moses is no longer alone, no longer without purpose. He is part of a people, and these people are dear to God's heart. God has heard their cries and suffering, and he calls Moses to bring him to this people.

WHO AM I?

Here's the big question that frames everything for Moses: "Who am I that I should go to Pharaoh, and bring the Israelites out of Egypt?" (Ex 3:11).

"Who am I?" The questions that the Scripture raises lay bare our deepest needs and insecurities, and certainly this big question of Moses is one of those times. We saw, in the first encounter between God and people in Genesis 3, God's first audible question to human beings: "Where are you?" (Gen 3:9). That question now finds its answer through Moses as he stands in the presence of the living God, unable to hide in the trees as the man and woman did in Genesis 3.

Yet even if he can't hide all of himself, he does hide his face in fear (Ex 3:6). In Hebrew, the word translated as "afraid" refers to a fear that opens us up to what is outside of us, making us realize our vulnerability, challenging us as to what sustains us. "I hate to say it," says novelist-essayist Marilynne Robinson in a review from the *New York Times*, but I think a default posture of human beings is fear. . . . What it comes down to—and I think this has become prominent in our culture recently—is that fear is an excuse: "I would like to have done something, but of course I couldn't." Fear is so opportunistic that people can call on it under the slightest provocations. . . . Fear has, in this moment, a respectability I've never seen in my life.[6]

Fear, as seen throughout the biblical account, will often take us in one of two directions. Fear either turns us to worship, because we realize we need to turn and bind our lives to God, or it makes us run in terror by going further and further into darkness. Fear brings out what is closest to us. When God calls you, what fear arises in you to push back? And do you run closer to God or further away? As we see in Exodus 3, Moses pushes back; he turns away from God and tries to hide. He sits at a crossroads at this moment, paralyzed by his own fear. But God answers his fear not by giving him rules, not by offering self-help talks, not through motivational statements that are on the sleeve of his Starbucks cup in the morning. Instead, he gives himself to Moses in a very specific way.

"I will be with you," God says, "and this shall be the sign for you that it is I who sent you: when you have brought the people out of Egypt, you shall worship God on this mountain" (Ex 3:12). God shows us that the address to mail our fears to is *worship*. If we hoard our fears into our souls, if we try to bury them under ourselves and step on them, they will gain a sickening, toxic place in our lives. But if we give them over to God in worship, if we turn our hands and our hearts and our faces to God, then we can let go of the fear and allow God to meet us. We can be *with* God in the fullest sense of the word.

Moses is now bound to God's people, as God is saying. He wants to form a new people. God wants to bring your fears and your identity not to a place of isolation but to one that is *with* the people—people who need you, people who need your gifts and your skills and your talents to be a blessing in their lives. Over and over again, this has been a theme of God throughout the Scriptures, and we're only in the second book of the Old Testament! And over and over again God is going to *be* the provision for God's people. God will meet us. God will be with us. God will strengthen us and care for us. It won't be easy, but God's provision will be there.

This peopling activity of God, this community he is creating moment by moment, is seen again much later in the Scriptures at the table of Communion. Jesus prepares for us to gather as a people as he remakes the Passover. As Jesus brings his disciples together in the upper room, it is during a time of great terror, of intense fear. *Will we survive?* the disciples might be wondering. *People are hunting for us. They want to kill you, Jesus. How can we possibly survive, and what are we supposed to do?* The people wanted to scatter. But around this table, the Lord *gathers* his people, pouring himself into this community, feeding them and binding them together in a new way, a peopling activity. "Do this in remembrance of me," he says, giving them his body (Lk 22:19). *Live out this practice together in remembrance of me.* Passover now becomes embrace and reconciliation.

The re-creating act that God does at the table, as he did with Moses at the burning bush, is to make a new reality where there was none before. Even though the common, mundane activities of life have gotten Moses into a rut, God, through a burning bush, breaks open new possibilities, giving Moses a renewed purpose, a deep calling. God binds Moses to himself and calls him into a people that he has forgotten amid his drudgery. Jesus does the same thing with his disciples: he calls them into a new reality and a new hope. This act of remaking, this recalling of what God is doing, is key to understanding not only what happens with Moses but with our lives as well. As God's people, in order for the life of God to really take hold, we have to allow God to take hold of us, grab onto us, shake us out of the mundane routines of our lives, and pull us up from the muck and mire, allowing us to become part of a people we may not know yet but God wants to call us into. That's what Moses is facing in the midst of this burning bush. He's being told by God to go meet new people, to have a renewed relationship with a people he's been estranged from for decades. Who wouldn't be terrified by that? *Who am I to do such a task?* Moses must be thinking to himself. And in this self-doubt, on this mountaintop, he is nonetheless called to leave behind the dark shadows of a broken and battered life.

SOMETIMES BURNING BUSHES COME IN
SHORT STORIES AND GENETICS LABS

I went to college with the expectation that I was going to be a chemistry major and eventually go to medical school. During my last two years in high school I was in a health science track, volunteering at the University of Washington Medical Center, and I felt like I had everything figured out. During my freshman year in college I jumped right into taking only STEM courses and spent hours in the lab. It was challenging, but I genuinely felt as if I was working on the path God had for me. My spring term I took a class called "Southern Writers," which I viewed primarily as a way to knock out a general education requirement. It was also my third quarter of chemistry and biology, which were highly lab intensive courses. This meant most of my Saturdays were taken up in front of fume hoods monitoring reactions to unknowns.

One of the texts we read in that southern writers class was a short story by Flannery O'Connor titled "Revelation." The main character is a woman named Ruby Turpin, who has her mind made up about the world. She has deep prejudices coupled with an aloofness that become threatened when she is attacked by a young girl named Mary Grace, who is surly and has acne, in a doctor's office. Mrs. Turpin looks down on Mary Grace for her ugliness, which results in Mary Grace hitting her with a human development textbook and calling her an "old wart hog."

Mrs. Turpin up to this point feels like she is doing everything right by God and humanity—being kind, following the rules, and focusing on making herself a better person. Yet she is shocked to find that she is neither truly listening to God nor seeing the world as God sees it. She begins to wonder if maybe Mary Grace is delivering a message from God and is shaking her to see anew. The story turns on Mrs. Turpin having a vision of the heavens where the last shall indeed be first and the first (such as Mrs. Turpin and those she has valued) will be last.

I had loved literature in high school but honestly never considered it as anything beyond a hobby. Yet this class turned my world upside down. I started to see the power of the arts to confront, to name, and to heal what it means to be human in ways I never thought possible. I realized that what I was looking for in my life—to ask big questions, to seek deeper understanding of what it means to be human, and to serve God with our whole heart, mind, and strength—were what the arts are about.

I still love science and teach many premed majors as a professor, but that Flannery O'Connor story was a burning bush in my life that shifted how I was looking at my sense of vocation and what I was being called to do, not only as a college student but with my life. Yet I had spent so many years invested in the dream of being a chemistry major and going to medical school that I didn't listen to the call from this burning bush. I went into my sophomore year determined to focus and double down on my drive in the sciences. I took more STEM courses, and it was in the midst of taking genetics that everything hit the wall. For my lab work I was paired with a friend who was not only excelling in the class but loving, I mean *loving*, the subject. He smiled and exhibited silent joy every time we were in the lab together. I distinctly remember looking across the table one day thinking, *Why don't I feel like that?* and then it hit me: I do feel that way in my English literature courses.

That term I was also taking Shakespeare, which met at 7:30 a.m. (an ungodly hour for any college course to be offered) and continued to come away from every class session—whether studying the tragedies, the comedies, or the sonnets—with another vision of humanity that I had never considered before. I simply couldn't get enough. It wasn't merely intellectual fascination but a true awakening in my heart that the arts and theology were my calling, and to share this with others would be an amazing way to spend my life. It was a hard journey to let go of my previous dreams and accept the new vision before me. To be honest I still have some doubts. But I know that the life given to me and the shift in not only my major but awakening to my calling to become a pastor and later a professor has been the right path.

My genetics lab partner? He is now the department chair of the biology department at the university where I teach. We often laugh about those days in the lab and how obvious our eventual paths were, even though it took a while to settle into God's train ride. But hindsight is indeed 20/20, and burning bushes do indeed show up if we pay attention, even in short stories and genetics labs.

The fear of making a change and the shame that is tapping you on the side of your head, those burdens you carry around with you—you have to let them go. "I'm going to take you to a new place," God is saying. "I'm going to bring you to these people, and you are going be a voice for them." How many of us drag the past with us and basically tell ourselves it's impossible for us to see God do something as mighty and amazing as that?

We need to remember that this is what God does and what God is calling us to, especially today. Recently the Social Security Administration reported that from this day forward, ten thousand people will turn sixty-five years old every day.[7] This wave of baby boomers changing into a new season of life also brings with it the possibility of a generation thinking, *Well, I'm done now. I've done everything that I can do, and I'm ready to move into a life of settling.* Moses is being asked *not* to do that. He's being called to a different life, a life of purpose and meaning, even though he's been around for eight decades.

Near the other end of the age spectrum, we have a generation mired under unbelievable debt and economic uncertainty. "What's the point of struggling?" they ask. "What's the point of going after jobs and dreams in a society like this anymore?" But God is saying, "Don't fall into the trap of the mundane! Don't give into the lure of numbing repetition! Allow me to get ahold of you and awaken new things!"

Brevard Childs says that one of the greatest themes running through Exodus is that God is making known his will and purpose such that we can discover that the divine is going to call us into a new way of being.[8] Moses' response to God does, in some ways, live into that idea—hence our grand question for this chapter: "What shall I say to them?" (Ex 3:13). After all of this, God breaking in, grabbing our attention, calling us out to this new thing, what then? What am I supposed to say in response to God's acts? What do I say to those in my care? How can I convince them?

In response, God gives his famous and rather strange statement about his name: "I AM WHO I AM" (Ex 3:14). God isn't saying that he's an inert statue that is fixed in the universe. Many Jewish scholars, including Martin Buber, have said a better translation would be, "I will be there as the one. I will be there as the one, I will be there."[9] God, Buber says, is the God being there, the God freeing, leading, going along, feeling with you, who is also unseasonable, at times unavailable, and a God you cannot make an image of. This "I AM" is the One who will be there with the people, with them in their suffering, a God on the move, not a God who is merely going to sit on a mountaintop, not a God who is fixed and locked in some particular place. This is a God who is going to move with us, who will give us purpose in what we do.

Moses' story also shows that God can use incomplete, broken people as part of his story. That's incredibly good news. "Grace," wrote Paul Tillich, strikes us when we are in great pain and restlessness. It strikes us when we walk through the dark valley of meaningless and empty life. . . . It strikes us when our disgust for our own being, our indifference, our weakness, our hostility, and our lack of direction and composure have become intolerable to us. It strikes us when, year after year, the longed-for perfection of life does not appear, when the old compulsions reign within us as they have for decades, when despair destroys all joy and courage. Sometimes at that moment a wave of light breaks into our darkness, and it is as though a voice were saying: "You are accepted. *You are accepted*, accepted by that which is greater than you, and the name of which you do not know. Do not ask for the name now; perhaps you will find it later. Do not try to do anything now; perhaps later you will do much. Do not seek for anything; do not perform anything; do not intend anything. Simply accept the fact that you are accepted!" . . . After such an experience we may not be better than before, and we may not believe better than before. But everything is transformed.[10]

As Moses experienced there at burning bush, you too are radically accepted: in your shame, in your brokenness, in the incompleteness of your life, in the dreams you have had up to this point that have not turned out the way you had hoped, and in your wandering, your seeking, and maybe even your resignation to the monotony of it all with the silent cry of, "Lord, just let me finish it out, please."

In his *Old Testament Theology in a Canonical Context*, Brevard Childs notes that "One of the great themes running throughout the book of Genesis is God's making known his will and purpose to the patriarchs as he breaks into their lives. . . . Similarly, Moses thought that he was discovering the divine, only to experience that he was being discovered."[11]

This is good news! While we may think the task of life is only to seek after answers, God shows us through the life of Moses that we not only seek but are being sought after by the great Redeemer and Sustainer of life everlasting. Are you open to the possibility that the Holy Spirit may have another chapter for you today? As Moses discovers on the mountaintop, our destiny is not a passive one in which we sit and wait for life to happen to us. We may think that we have everything figured out, but God breaks in at the strangest times and most startling ways. What an adventure awaits us when we are open to what God has in store, whether on the mountaintop or in the valley!

5

WHY THIS BURDEN?

Questions of Burdens and Doubts

Where there is charity and wisdom, there is neither fear
nor ignorance. Where there is patience and humility, there
is neither anger nor vexation. Where there is poverty
and joy, there is neither greed nor avarice. Where there is
peace and mediation, there is neither anxiety nor doubt.

ST. FRANCIS OF ASSISI
THE COUNSELS OF THE HOLY FATHER ST. FRANCIS

Whether movie catch phrases, advertisements, or social media viral memes, there seems to be no shortage of pithy statements that attempt to sum up the human condition. Driving to my parents' retirement home a few weeks ago, a billboard showed a man with a wry smile on his face while operating a riding lawn mower across a beautifully landscaped yard with the caption, "Life Is Hard. Deal with It." Underneath the billboard sat a man at the stoplight holding a cardboard sign reading, "Life is really hard. I don't have a yard. $$$ please." The juxtaposition was powerful.

I am not sure how many people driving by made the connection, but I was taken with how often the words we use to describe pain and loss and disappointment can fall flat once they are put into the larger context of human tragedy. The two-dimensional airbrushed advertisement was selling a particular vision of life where the biggest problem was how to tame a lawn on a large estate, and the solution could be delivered to my doorstep with a simple online purchase. Yet the all-too-real three-dimensional truth was sitting just below on the street in front of us as a very real human who accurately captured what it means to say "life is hard."

Yet sometimes we can view challenges and difficulties of others and assume that it is all sorrow when they have a life that is different than ours. This is often the case in cultural stereotypes of rural areas—where people living close to the land free of Wi-Fi, video streaming, SUVs, Amazon Prime delivery, and smartphones couldn't possibly be living the good life. This can also extend to how we view other people who might have physical and mental challenges distinct from our own.

This summer my daughter worked as a counselor at Special Friends camp, which is a week-long day and overnight camping experience for older adults with Down syndrome, autism, and other challenges. While there are many camps for children with special challenges, there are few for adults who have a childlike wonder and desire a time of fun, fellowship, and adventure apart from their day-to-day caregivers. These adults ranging in age from nineteen to seventy-two laughed, sang camp songs, worked with horses, and did skits and challenge courses with all the zest and zeal of anyone who has fully and completely experienced the joy of the outdoors and God's wonder in community. One young man with cerebral palsy spent one entire afternoon simply floating in the pool and feeling the water lift him free with a smile of joy and contentment from ear to ear. An older woman who is both deaf and blind laughed aloud as the whoosh of air and the thrill of movement on her skin embraced her as she zoomed along a zip line.

It was a week of fourteen-hour days for my daughter and the other counselors at the camp. I was frankly worried as I drove to pick her up at the end of the week, thinking she would be physically and psychologically wrecked. But as I drove in to the camp, the energy was palpable. True, it was evident that it had been a busy, full, and at times exhausting week. But all the counselors had looks on their faces that are rarely seen when I walk downtown and see workers rushing and shoving their way into IT work farms and skyscrapers, so unlike dull eyes of drivers stuck on the freeway (to paraphrase an old Police song) like lemmings crammed into shiny metal boxes.

These counselors had worked hard, were physically tired, but they also had a sense of purpose, contentment, and fulfilment that lit up their eyes and put smiles on their faces. Their lives had connected with meaning, and they had been within a community that had no filters, no cynicism, no speculation as to each other's motives. It was a week of people saying exactly what they thought and felt and not hiding their joys, fears, or sorrows. When a camper told you that you were beautiful, that they loved you, that they needed help, and that they would miss you, you had no reason to doubt the truth because this was a community that didn't hide themselves.

As my daughter reflected on our way home, she saw more of Jesus during that week than she had in a year of Sundays. What some might have seen as a burdensome week—fourteen-hour days with high-need individuals—was actually a transformative and spirit-filling encounter that changed her life.

What makes something a burden is not merely a matter of a frame of mind or whether we buy the right riding lawnmower. An honest appraisal of life includes the reality of difficulty, challenges, pain, suffering, disappointment, loss, and heartbreak. Burdens are part of life. Yet with the burdens given us, we should acknowledge that we are also surrounded by much more than the weight and pain we experience. In order to discover the height and breadth and depth of life in all its fullness, we should look at our burdens with clear eyes but also in the context of how large our lives are, the community surrounding us, and the God who stands at our side.

WILDERNESS SHOWS US OUR NATURE
IN THE MIDST OF GOD'S CREATION

Looking at the life of Moses, we find that he asks the question of life's burdens as well. It's important to remember that he is asking this in the wilderness, which leads us to an important idea: *the wildernesses of life will expose us to what is essential in life.* It's precisely in the wilderness that we will discover what burdens we carry, what burdens exist in the lives of those around us, and what burdens are on God's heart. As we'll see, the burdens that Moses carries and that the Israelites carry are not very different from the burdens we bear today.

When people reflect on what God is doing in the grandeur of his plan, it's hard to reduce it to essentials. In the Talmud, which is a commentary that ancient rabbis used to gather their thoughts as they prepared to teach, there's a debate about how to boil down all the complexities of what God has asked us.

During the debate, a rabbi raises his hand and says that the summation of all the duties is very simple: we simply need to obey the 613 laws given by Moses to Israel, and that will be that. Another rabbi says that he thinks it can be simpler than that: we just need to look at what David did in Psalm 15 and reduce it to eleven principles. Now we've gone from 613 commands to a much more manageable 11. But another rabbi then turns and says that actually, Micah gave it to us: Micah 6:8 says to do justice, love kindness, and walk humbly with God—*three* basic things. But another rabbi speaks up and points to Isaiah 56:1, in which we have but *two* principles: "Thus says the LORD: Maintain justice, and do what is right." As the rabbis continue debating, Rabbi Ben Isaac stands up and says it's all far too complex. What we have in the Scriptures and what God has taught us, he says, is a very basic thing, summarized in Habakkuk 2:4: "The righteous live by their faith."[1]

At last, we have one single thing! "The righteous live by their faith." By depending on God's faithfulness to us, all other things fall into place. The idea that the righteous will live by their faithfulness runs through all of our Scriptures, including in the New Testament. Romans 1:17 cites the Habakkuk passage, as do Galatians 3:11 and Hebrews 10:38. It's a refrain throughout the text, and it changed history. Martin Luther, a young Augustinian monk, reflecting on the Romans passage, lifted his head up from the Scriptures and changed the way the church understood itself in the modern period. In the twentieth century, with National Socialism on the rise after World War I, Karl Barth, a young pastor, reflected on the epistle to the Romans and read for himself that by faithfulness the righteous will live. Barth saw in the book of Romans a call to faithful action. Taking up social activism for the sake of the gospel, he went out to the coal mines and the villages where he'd been pastoring and proclaimed the centrality of the cross and the call to repentance. He ultimately transformed New Testament scholarship, calling people to rediscover the cross with renewed passion and faith.

Do we as people in the twenty-first century understand that the righteous, by our faithfulness in God's faithfulness, will live? Do we trust in God fully? Where do you sit in relation to this call?

The question of how we live by God's righteousness is central to how we face burdens in our lives and how we live through wilderness times. The book of Numbers is entirely a wilderness narrative, the whole of the text taking place in the desert while Israel is waiting to enter the Promised Land. Wilderness is an important picture to keep in mind with regard to Scripture. The definition of wilderness isn't just about getting your season pass and going for a hike on the Pacific Crest Trail like John Muir. *Wilderness in Scripture is something more: it denotes a place where the people can only survive because of God's provision.* It's where you are when your survival absolutely depends on God's action. It's not a place where you can go and plant seeds and expect to grow crops and say, "Look what I did!" It doesn't have manicured paths you can stroll while taking selfies for your social media feed. In this context, wilderness is a brutal place, a place where our only resort is to lean heavily, completely, utterly on the provision of God.

In the first ten chapters of Numbers, Israel is moving from the wilderness of Sinai toward a new place. Earlier in the narrative, when Moses receives his call at the burning bush, God breaks his centuries-long silence to the people of Israel, showing himself to be alive, working alongside the people of Israel, calling Moses to action to unite his people and lead them to freedom. In Numbers, Moses goes a step further and calls them together in a camp meeting. There they bind together as a unified *people* of the living God. God is going to be *with* the people, the people Israel, and lead them, and call them. It's here at Sinai, the place where God meets them, where the people tangibly experience God's provision in the covenant community that is formed and sustained by the God who never left them and never will.

The covenant is established, Israel is on the move, and they're following God, but when we pick up the action here in Numbers, they have been wandering for two long years. The cloud is indeed moving them, and they're following, and God has been providing for their needs, but the ordeal is exhausting. Every day, the people pick up and move again, and they move again, and they move again. Along the way, the people start complaining— whining that what they're getting isn't enough. That brings us to the first burden: nostalgia.

THE BURDEN OF NOSTALGIA

Here at the beginning of Numbers, the people are complaining about their diet, lamenting the food they have been given every day by the miraculous providence of God (see Ex 16:12-15). But the particular foods that they *haven't* been given are what they remember from their years back in Egypt: "We remember the fish we used to eat in Egypt for nothing," they complain, "the cucumbers, the melons, the leeks, the onions, and the garlic" (Num 11:5). The era of bondage from back before they were set free now holds a place of longing in their hearts. As they travel, their question "Why did we ever leave Egypt?" (Num 11:20) seems to go on and on like a bad pop song that you just can't get out of your head.

It's a strange encounter when you think about it. These people had been beaten and tortured as slaves, and now, even though they've been set free, they're thinking fondly of how good life was in Egypt. If I'm honest, I have to admit that the idea of an Egyptian diet sounds kind of good. But to go back to a place of slavery? Why would anyone want to do that?

What Moses is trying to deal with, what the people are dealing with, isn't the reality of their past but a *romanticized* version of their past. They are looking back to a time when life was certain, when they could count on exactly what was going to happen every minute of every day. Even if it was painful and even if it was awful, it's certainty that they now want. Faith has become exhausting; certainty, even enslaved certainty, seems better than what they are experiencing right now.

Why do we go back to the things that imprison us? What is it about the romance of the past that we want to return to, even when we know it'll destroy us? In his book *This Is Your Brain on Music: The Science of a Human Obsession*, Daniel J. Levitin describes why we fall in love with pop music. Why is it that forty years later, we can hear a song in the supermarket or on an elevator and be brought right back to the moment we first heard the song? Why do we lock in to particular types of music, wanting to keep them for ourselves and our soundtracks and our playlists? What happens in us?[2]

Studying the brain's pleasure centers, Levitin says that large amounts of dopamine and serotonin are released when we experience something that makes us joyful. When the pleasure centers get fired up and various chemicals are released, what we experience gets tied in to our neural pathways with a feeling not only of joy and ecstasy but of safety and peace.

A similar thing happens with foods as well, as in the romance we feel when we remember the Thanksgiving Day table, a Christmas meal, a summer picnic, or a good barbecue. Calling these things to mind elicits something in us, and we release all these pleasure chemicals in our brain. There's something about a romantic recollection of a fond memory that makes us think that nothing can go wrong. We don't think about how we had to swat away the wasps at the barbecue or about the grumblings that happened in the kitchen during the Thanksgiving meal when our parents didn't understand us. No, those things are diminished under a sea of chemical stimulation, and we end up romanticizing that past, re-creating it as a memory of safety, peace, and uninterrupted pleasure.

That's what's happening with Israel at this point in Numbers. They've forgotten that the scars on their backs came from a particular place. They have forgotten the cost of getting to where they are. They would rather live in the past—in a memory that has been sanitized of pain and suffering and made falsely into a place of certainty and provision—than to face the reality of day-in, day-out dependence on the intimacy of God. Nostalgia has become a fortress for Israel and is blocking out what God is trying to provide for them in the form of a new future.

I WISH I WAS A SLAVE TO AN AGE-OLD TRADE

The burden of nostalgia can be our story too. It's certainly been my story at various times. I find myself going through seasons of stress in my life, thinking about work nonstop, fixating on all the busyness in my life, craving a retreat to simpler times. The band The Head and the Heart has a song titled "Down in the Valley" that begins with the line, "I wish I was a slave to an age-old trade / Like ridin' around on railcars and workin' long days."[3] It is a song of such powerful longing for simpler times that workers in cubicles, getting hourly wages that can barely pay rent, made it a big hit. I think that each of us has a go-to, simpler fantasy narrative that helps us get through life a little more easily, like riding around on railcars in some idyllic past. What has been your particular burden of nostalgia? What nostalgia do you retreat to in order to avoid the reality of what God is calling you to? What mental images, what yearnings for a bygone time or season of life tempt you to try to evade God's journey for your life? Maybe someone's image will come up on your social media newsfeed and you'll find yourself thinking, *Ah, that high school crush from back when I was a teenager. Maybe if I had made a move in her direction, my life would be better now, not like this hard marriage that I'm in.* Or, *If I had gone to a different college, maybe my career would be a better story. What if I had taken a left instead of a right? What if I had pursued* x *friendship over* y *friendship? What if I had taken* that *job instead of* this *one? What if I were in a different church, where people understood me, rather than this one where they don't even play the music I like?*

The burden of nostalgia is not merely an individualistic longing. We see this played out communally, culturally, and nationally. People have certain nostalgic mythologies of what life was back in the nineteenth century or even in the 1950s that have more to do with the media depictions of *Downton Abbey*, Jane Austen novels, *Little House on the Prairie*, *Anne of Green Gables*, *Leave It to Beaver*, or *Mad Men* than actual reality. This is especially true with notions of making America great again in politics, which are pretty selective about what was great and for whom, whether under slavery or Jim Crow or the like. History, as they say, is told and retold by the so-called victors, which is why nostalgic narratives take hold and have such political and cultural power.

We each have narratives calling to us like Sirens calling to Odysseus, tempting us to forsake the adventure God has called us to in exchange for a counterfeit version of "what could have been." But fascinations with the past can lock us in place and prevent us from seeing what God is trying to do in the present. Which brings us back to the groaning of Israel.

THE BURDEN OF LEADERSHIP

In Numbers 11:11-13 Moses offers a series of questions that frame many of the challenges faced by leaders in the midst of difficulties. "Why have you brought this trouble on your servant?" (NIV) is a question that places blame on God in a way that seeks resolution to the reality of why suffering happens to well-meaning people. Whereas "What have I done to displease you?" is a question of self-doubt, self-blame, and a sense of failure or inadequacy, "Where can I get meat for all these people?" is a practical question of logistics, but more significantly a deeper question of faith and provision. This series of questions cascades from Moses like a torrent and gives honest evidence to the real questions leaders face in times of crisis. This shows us that when things go wrong, we ask questions of God and of ourselves. We doubt our calling, our ability, and God's capacity to fulfill what he's asked us to do.

Needless to say I can relate to Moses, as can many others when faced with the challenges of leadership. Prior to teaching at the University of Glasgow, I was assistant minister at the Glasgow Cathedral. Founded in 1136, the High Kirk of Glasgow is a large Gothic cathedral that is in many ways the center of culture and civic life for West Scotland. As one of the Queen's chapels in the United Kingdom, it is the place where the royal family attends high services when in Scotland. Among my duties as a minister of the cathedral I led a midweek prayer service. The tradition of leading the midweek service goes back to the Victorian period as a way to ensure that the work week was afforded a time of reflection on God's providence and grace. Each Wednesday, workers throughout the city would take off work at 11 a.m. and come to a short time of prayer and Scripture reading.

Given the grand size of the cathedral both in the sanctuary and the nave, it was easy to imagine the numbers of people filling the space over the decades. Yet the numbers gathering for midweek prayers in the twenty-first century primarily came for different reasons. Busloads of tourists coming to the city often arrived in this historic space right as the midweek prayers began. Given that I was in full cassock and ministerial vestments and framed by the Gothic interiors, it made for something of a period drama.

The first few weeks I was shocked to find that many people in the pews had their cameras and phones out to take pictures and record the service rather than participate in the liturgy, some even putting away their recording devices once they heard that I didn't have a Scottish brogue! It was disheartening to think that people weren't necessarily gathering to use the time to sit and worship God, as I had hoped they would. But I also realized that I had perhaps romanticized the generations of those who gathered in this space over the centuries and afforded them a level of pious resolve that just wasn't fair. In short, no one comes to church with the purest of motives, including the clergy! Initially I was frustrated and even wondered aloud to my wife if it was worth showing up. But it became clear that I wasn't there for them alone but for the worship of God no matter who showed up.

There was one Wednesday in particular during the winter when no one showed up, and I realized that I needed to lead the liturgy of the day regardless of the empty pews. My calling in that space and at that time was to pray, so pray I did. I believe in this regard that Moses offers us a portrait for both leaders and members of communities to learn from. People crowd around us for reasons far afield from the pure and righteous motives we may wish them to have. They may come clamoring for things out of our control—whether it be fresh produce in the desert or a Scottish accent to fulfill their vacation Snapchat—but the calling of leaders is to lead with patience and humility nonetheless.

THE BURDEN OF COMMUNITY

As Moses listens to the rabble-rousing and complaining about how great it would be to go back to Egypt, he finally gets so overwhelmed with the task of keeping Israel focused that he turns to the Lord for help. "I am not able to carry all this people alone," he laments, "for they are too heavy for me" (Num 11:14). Moses is isolated, and his reaction is to declare that he doesn't want these people anymore. He doesn't think these people are even *his* people any longer. He's completely changed his tune from Exodus 3. Back then, God had been binding him to the Hebrew people, calling him to lead them out of slavery into a new life of freedom. But here, a few short years later, he's essentially done an about-face. "These are not my people," we can almost hear him saying to the Lord. "God, *you* created them. You're the mother that is supposed to be feeding them. Take care of them! What am I supposed to do? Am I a Walmart Supercenter? Can I provide them leeks and cucumbers? These people are driving me crazy!" Moses is saying, "Just kill me now! Put me out of my misery!"

And the burden Moses is feeling is the reality that communities of people are difficult. It's difficult to live with other people. How often have we experienced that in our own lives and churches when we've been confronted with other people's brokenness, sin, and needlessly small-minded visions? How often have we shown those things *ourselves*? Moses is making a similar move to what Cain did by distancing himself from Abel: "Am I my brother's keeper?" (Gen 4:9). "Am I really related to this person? Do I really have to care for her? Because, God, that's your job, not mine! I don't have any burden of caring for this person, for that church, for these situations!" Moses is saying the exact same thing: Am I even connected to them? Are these people my people? Are they really my responsibility? Why have you put this burden on me to even think about?

What Moses is doing here allows us to look into our own lives in two important ways. First, how easy is it to blame our problems on other people? *If I had different friends*, we think. Or *If I had a different marriage, if I had a different home life, if I had different people on my dorm floor—then my problems would go away. I would be a better person if* so-and-so *weren't in my life*. It's a way for us to evade responsibility for our own lives.

Second, this story shows that we can blame *other people's problems* on someone else too. *If someone else would just take care of those people, then everything would be fine—but who am I to deal with that?* A few years back, when my family and I were living in Scotland, there was a fascinating BBC radio show dealing with how people search for God. This was during a time when New Atheism was gaining in popularity—think Richard Dawkins and Christopher Hitchens. On the show, the reporters interviewed people on the streets of London, asking what they believed about God, and when an interviewee said they were an atheist, the reporters would ask why. Several of the people used the example of the rise of HIV/AIDS in African countries. "If you look at what's going on in Africa right now with the rise of AIDS," they were essentially saying, "how can there possibly be a God? If there is a God, he's obviously not caring for them, so how could I possibly be expected to believe that God is real?"

So the BBC team went to Malawi, a place where HIV has wiped out entire generations with 14 percent of its twelve million people being HIV-positive, but which also has a large Christian population with over half of the population being Protestant and another 20 percent Roman Catholic, as the reporters discovered when they visited churches that featured people singing, clapping, and literally dancing in the aisles.[4] As they interviewed worshipers, they asked them what they thought of the fact that some Londoners said that the goings-on in places like this was the reason why they couldn't believe in God. One man, stepping back from the microphone in surprise, said, "Look around! If God is not there" (meaning in England), "they should come here! For God is with us. God has met us here. God has been with us; in the midst of our suffering God is here."

And that's what Moses and the Israelites are missing at this moment in Numbers. They are so focused on their issues, on their nostalgic view of the past, on the particularities of their wants and desires, that they don't hear that God is in the wilderness, still trying to break through and nourish them in new ways.

Much later, in the New Testament, Jesus' wilderness wanderings provide another lens through which we can look at the Moses story. While Israel grumbles and complains about their wilderness experience, Jesus goes in *willingly* (see Mt 4). Even though he's tempted by Satan in every way, Jesus chooses to rely heavily on the provisions of God instead of trying to divert his attention elsewhere as Moses and the Israelites did. Jesus' model of wilderness wandering is that God provides sustenance, even though it sometimes takes a while to get the full view of what God has in store. By end of the narrative, "the devil left him, and suddenly angels came and waited on him" (Mt 4:11). Jesus shows us that the wilderness seasons aren't about being alone and soldiering alone. Instead, the wilderness time is about leaning into those God puts around us—waiting patiently for the moment when God will act and refusing to blame others for what we're experiencing.

THE BURDEN OF COVENANT

The third thing that the Numbers narrative teaches us has to do with the burden of covenant. The community of God's people can be difficult, hard to work with, taxing to tolerate, laborious to listen to. Israel demonstrates that just because we are chosen by God doesn't mean that things will be easy or pain free, but we will have purpose and companionship through the joy and pain. Pain "removes the veil," wrote C. S. Lewis in *The Problem of Pain*. "It plants the flag of truth within the fortress of a rebel soul."[5] The sufferings of the wilderness will expose our life. The wilderness that we are in right now, that we've gone through, will help us to see exactly what it is that we rely on to get by—whether it's God, something else, or some mixture of God and other things. It's not that we should *choose* pain and suffering, nor should we valorize it, as though it's some kind of badge of honor to pick pain for its own sake. But when the difficult seasons of wilderness *do* come, we have a chance to listen even more deeply to God's covenant story with us—to remember that God's provision is deep, abiding, and consistent, even though it often takes time to realize completely. Numbers isn't a journalistic account; it was written long *after* Israel's wanderings, as a reflection back on how God had shown his faithfulness (Num 36:13) and for us to listen to today. On our end of history, we know that Israel *will* get to the Promised Land. But we also know how much it's going to cost them to get there. Lives will be lost. There will be suffering. It will be painful. But God is going to be there with them every step of the way. And when Jesus arrives, announcing the coming kingdom, he will suffer and die, but come back again, walking with us in our suffering and our wilderness as one who has been there himself and triumphed.

We need to remember these things because God's covenant isn't a quick fix: it's a *long-term* journey. God's timing is perfect, and in the meantime the righteous, by his faithfulness, will indeed live (Hab 2:4). This is the truth that the rabbis were getting at while they looked at the text and debated it among themselves. It's what we're called to listen to today as we encounter Numbers 11.

In the end, the faithfulness of God does save Moses and the people of Israel. God takes God's Spirit, what had been burdening Moses, and breathes it into the seventy leaders around him—dispersing God's own person *into* the community around Moses, spreading the burden out from one person into an entire cohort of leaders. God himself is bearing the burden in the midst of the community (Num 11:16-25).

God's provision will ultimately free us. Nostalgia for the past is not going to free you. It will trap you, entangle you, and get you off focus, wishing for something that cannot be. It's in *this* life, in *this* place, in *this* day, that Jesus wants to meet you, surrounded by the realness of your suffering and pain, desiring to bring you something to help you get through to the promised land he has for you. It might not taste as good as a cucumber or a melon, but if you're ready to wait for it, God has in store for you a vast banquet of the finest food. The community God is forming and forging through it all will be the people that God himself will inhabit.

In this room, in this place, in your reading this now, know that God doesn't desire you to be alone in your burden. The covenant of God is *for* God's people, not against them, as though he would ever lose them. We are not alone; we are not destitute by ourselves; the burden we feel on our shoulders isn't ours to carry on our own. We have each other, God's covenant people, to get us through the wilderness to the promised land. God's breath blows into those in the community around you if you're willing to be invested in them, so they can be invested in you. Let others get close to you—to know your heart, to know your pain, to help you not to be in isolation anymore.

Elsewhere in Numbers God gives this blessing to the people of Israel,

> The LORD bless you and keep you;
> the LORD make his face to shine upon you, and be
>   gracious to you;
> the LORD lift up his countenance upon you, and give you
>   peace. (Num 6:24-26)

Before you and I are ever tempted to succumb to the grumblings and the rabble-rousing and the burden, God has said, "I will bless you. It's going to be hard, but my face will be for you to provide for you and to care for you." This promise is ours today. Moses learns to be faithful to God's call despite his perception of circumstances and softens his heart to the people who surround him even in the midst of their grumbling. This is difficult and requires Moses to humble himself in profound ways. This softening of heart and refocusing on his mission comes through his willingness to question God and allow that open heartbreak to be filled by God's challenge and provision.

The burden of nostalgia ultimately breeds a (mis)remembering of the past. The burden of leadership and community acknowledges the challenges we face in living and working with others. The burden of covenant reveals our tendency to not trust the hope found in the future and perhaps give up too soon and retreat back to old, familiar ways that, while painful, at least give us a sense of control by returning to whatever Egypt we may be fleeing. Yet the covenant of God is still alive and well, as Moses discovers once he lets God respond to his deep question "Why this burden?"

This is not to say that all will turn out as we might hope, since God's hope is larger and more expansive than our own and therefore will sometimes include disappointment prior to understanding and peace. Moses himself (spoiler alert) was not able to enter the Promised Land he worked so hard to lead the people to. In the end, the journey was the destination, and his chapter closed as he looked into a land he would never inherit himself. But Moses found a place for his burdens in submitting to God's responses to his question, and that changed his need to give up burdens. Rather, he found purpose and peace in the midst of burdens.

Where are you in this journey alongside Moses? As you consider the burdens in your life, how do they align with Moses? In what ways do you find peace in the times of trial, and what questions about your burdens do you wish to ask of God now? As we see in Numbers, God's breath has blown through you, as it did in Moses' life, to bear the burdens of your soul. What will you do to receive the blessing he has for you today?

6

HOW CAN I JUST VANISH
IN DARKNESS?

Questions of Loss, Conviction, and Work

I shall be telling this with a sigh
Somewhere ages and ages hence . . .

ROBERT FROST
"THE ROAD NOT TAKEN"

No matter what . . . it is with God. He is gracious
and merciful. His way is in love, through which
we all are. It is truly— a love supreme.

JOHN COLTRANE
LINER NOTES FOR *A LOVE SUPREME*

D ave Eggers exploded onto the literary scene with his
memoir, *A Heartbreaking Work of Staggering Genius*, which
became a finalist for the Pulitzer Prize in nonfiction. The book
is worthy of its audacious title: it's a playful, sorrowful, imagi-
native memoir of a twenty-one-year-old man enduring the
sudden death of his father from brain and lung cancer, followed
thirty-two days later by the death of his mother from stomach

cancer. The memoir follows Eggers as he is left to raise his eight-year-old brother on his own while also struggling to come to terms with the death of his parents. He writes about having to grow up quickly in ways he hadn't anticipated, which involved giving up his dreams of staying forever young in the present and the visions he had for what his future would look like.[1]

Eggers's solution to the tragedy in his life strikes me in two ways. On the one hand, it seems laudable—channeling his pain and loss, as he does, into art and creativity that inspires others. (He currently runs a nonprofit in California that helps troubled youth learn creative writing.) But at the same time, the tone of the book itself seems like an all-too-familiar story of brashness and cynicism, the sort that deadens our feelings through irony, mean-spiritedness, and bravado. Throughout the book, Eggers chides others for not being as bright as he is and for not adopting his view of life, and he chooses to block himself off from others, including his extended family. In the end, I struggle with Eggers because even though he proves himself to be a multitalented artist, he's also pretty committed to the idea that the world is a cold, hard place, and that the way through it is to be true to yourself, to your own singular vision, and to laugh a lot at yourself and at others along the way.

Is Eggers's mode of life in the twenty-first century really the best option? Yes, we are living in a world in which well-educated, omnicapable young adults are struggling to make their way in a world with upside-down mortgages, limited job prospects, and wars and rumors of wars echoing in their ears. But if people don't like our way of doing things, is it really the best option just to steel ourselves against those around us and forge onward in spite of them?

The book of Job tells a story very similar to Eggers's in its tragedy, at least at first. Job is well known to Jews, Christians, and Muslims, as he is a prophet in all three of the Abrahamic religions, and his story represents one of the most widely known tales in literature: a story of such loss and torment that his very name is associated with the gravest moments of human grief. When someone has gone through unspeakable tragedy, it's common to evoke Job as a sacred hyperlink to help someone interpret what they're experiencing.

Job is the focus of a grand bargain between the God of Abraham, Isaac, and Jacob, and *ha satan*, the Hebrew term for "accuser," from which we derive the name Satan. The accuser brings cases against us on a regular basis, whispering in our ear ideas like, "You do not deserve your life," and "It's all a fraud. At any moment people will see through the smokescreen, through the blur of frenetic activity and noise, to see you for what you really are—and God knows the truth."

Job's life is framed by the grandest cosmic wager of all. The accuser goes to God with a fairly basic premise, which runs something like this: "Let's see what Job's faith is truly based on, shall we? Sure, under your protective and sustaining gaze, Job has been faithful. That's easy. But honestly, is that truly faith? Give Job to me and let's see how long he remains faithful" (compare Job 1:10-11).

So God lifts his hand of providence, and the accuser repeatedly afflicts him. His body is covered with boils, his home is destroyed, and his family dies—all at the same moment, all in the first two chapters of the book. The bulk of the remaining forty chapters of text are concerned with how Job deals with his tragedy, through the lens of conversations with his friends

Eliphaz, Bildad, and Zophar, and ultimately with God himself. He cries out:

> If I go forward, he is not there;
> or backward, I cannot perceive him;
> on the left he hides, and I cannot behold him;
> I turn to the right, but I cannot see him. (Job 23:8-9)

In the midst of Job's cascading, gut-wrenching lamentation (and the utterly unhelpful advice of his friends), we find Job's big question, which is a self-reflective, self-negating one: "If only I could vanish in darkness, / and thick darkness would cover my face!" (Job 23:17). Wondering aloud to himself as well as to God, Job acknowledges that the trauma and tragedy in his world is not a fiction, and he hopes for some clouding of his senses so at least he can be spared this reality. This is an exclamation that many of us can relate to. How do we make sense of tragedy, loss, and the seeming absence of God? When the trauma is so real and the loss so heartbreaking, we cannot deny the pain and still cry out for solace. This is the classic question of humanity: How do we make sense of suffering and our role in it?

In response, we see two options take shape in Job's story, which we often parallel in our own: we can either hold fast to a search for finding some reason for the suffering as a map through life and adhere to it so we can feel some sense of control, or we can become indifferent to the world and to others, choosing cynicism, irony, and flippancy as a way of protecting ourselves from pain.

For Job's friends, *the search for a reason behind suffering* is the best route. To Eliphaz, Bildad, and Zophar, Job's situation is fairly straightforward: pain and suffering have to have a reason, they say. What kind of universe would we be living in if suffering made no reasonable sense? Job, faithful to God and to his family, loses his wife, his children, his property, and his health, and seems to get no response to his cries. The three friends never waver from their belief that Job must have sinned somehow in order to incite God's punishment over him.

A New Testament parallel to that idea is found in the accusations leveled against the man born blind from birth, as those around him continually ask whose sin caused him to be born blind (see Jn 9). Job's friends berate him for refusing to confess his sins, even though they themselves are at a loss to explain exactly what sin he has committed. They also assume that God always rewards good and punishes evil, apparently with no exceptions allowed. There seems to be no room in their understanding of God for the idea of divine discretion and mystery in allowing and arranging suffering—that God could permit or even incite suffering for purposes other than retribution.

Hard-line thinking like that is grounded on the pragmatic view that life is always reasonable at some level. If we think hard enough, work hard enough, and are morally upright, we'll experience the good life. Are you poor? Destitute? Ask yourself: Did you deserve it? Are you unable to get a job? Have you not found the love of your life? Then for crying out loud, what are you doing wrong?

Such is the thinking of Job's three friends who seek reasonable explanations for suffering. But they also offer a second, equally bankrupt option: cynicism and irony. To adopt such a stance is to engage in what C. S. Lewis calls "the habit of flippancy"—indifference toward everything, a laughing-off of the problems of this life.[2] From where Job was sitting, scraping his withering flesh with a potsherd while sitting in the dust, flippancy might seem pretty inviting. Eliphaz, Bildad, and Zophar only make this option seem more attractive. "If God doesn't answer you," they essentially tell Job, "then just give up on God." It's secular humanism in its purest form: if the world doesn't operate in ways we can discern, that we can manage, that we can reasonably understand, then walk away from it.

A flippant view of God is the all-too-easy path of the New Atheism espoused by people like Christopher Hitchens and Richard Dawkins, or of folks who believe like Karl Marx that religion is "the sigh of the oppressed creature, the heart of a heartless world, and the soul of soulless conditions. It is the opium of the people."[3] Flippancy views God as a fairy tale that calls us to fly away on the power of wishful thinking, perhaps like Peter Pan, without taking seriously the trauma that breaks the hearts of the world's poor and destitute. Yet even Peter Pan found out that without his shadow he was never truly complete and whole. So it is with how we deal with suffering and disappointment. Rather than ask to be surrounded by a darkness that blinds us, as Job does, perhaps the path is to find our way into and through the darkness that is always part of life.

But Job chooses neither reasonableness alone nor cynicism. In Job 19, he declares his credo that "I know that my Redeemer lives" (v. 25), in so doing committing himself to the difficult place of accepting that God is not, as the hymn goes, "dead nor doth He sleep."[4] Quite the opposite: God isn't dead, and he's more than just a painkiller. God is real enough for Satan and therefore is certainly real enough for Job. To deny this would be to deny what it means to be in this world, even if the depth of this reality is deeper and darker than Job can see. By chapter 23, Job is at a crossroads, having heard all the arguments swirling around the problem of pain in this life from his so-called friends with their warped understanding of how religious life is supposed to work in a perfect world: do good, good things happen to you; do bad, bad will come to you. But rather than merely sitting and stewing in despair, Job rises up and journeys forth, possessing neither a map of certainty nor a laugh track of irony to accompany him.

> Oh, that I knew where I might find him,
>   that I might come even to his dwelling!
> I would lay my case before him,
>   and fill my mouth with arguments. (Job 23:3-4)

How do we navigate approaching God, given Job's example? How do we acknowledge that suffering is real—for Job, for us, for Dave Eggers—while also choosing not to give in to either certainty or cynicism?

THE REALITY OF HEARTBREAK

First, we have to accept the reality of heartbreak. To truly go to where God is, to accept what God has in store for us, is to acknowledge that our hearts will feel heavy at times. Job walks forth into the wilderness of his world as a broken man. That's neither stoicism nor denial, but instead it's an acknowledgment on Job's part that his heart might be broken yet again but that it's still worth it to get off the mat. His cry of "Oh that" (Job 23:3) is a textual marker and refrain that appears more often in Job than in any other book of the Hebrew Bible. It's an exclamation of hope in the face of hopelessness, yet it is a hope that risks disappointment. It will be extremely hard to leave your heart open to heartbreak in the days and years to come. Yet to live into the possibility of what God has in store, the journey will include the potential for heartbreak and an encounter with suffering.

"Americans have an anemic understanding of suffering and loss and a rabid fear of pain," said a retired missionary to a friend of mine. But Job has to give up his sense of security in order to move forward. In the New Testament, too, each of the disciples has to leave something behind in order to follow Jesus: Matthew leaves behind his tax table (Mt 9:9), the fishermen leave behind their nets (Mt 4:18-20), those who have been privileged leave behind status (Phil 3:7), those who are victims and broken are called into healing and have to leave their identity as victims in order to walk as redeemed and healed people (Jn 9).

Our culture teaches us that pain is to be avoided at all costs, even if the pain could be a path to our ultimate freedom. But can we stand up like Job, face the potential for heartbreak, and walk into God's future with confidence? St. Augustine's great cry in his *Confessions* was this simple refrain: "Our hearts find no peace until they rest in you."[5]

THE NECESSITY OF WORK

Second, to face life honestly and fully means accepting the necessity of work as separate from suffering. Job gets up from the dust of his broken life and gets to work seeking out whatever God has for him. It is not easy, but the work and calling on his life is not his suffering. In his conversations with his friends, he literally doesn't get anywhere. There is talk and more talk and more talk. While we need to have seasons for reflection, there is also a need for action and work. One of my students in a journal response was talking about his frustrations with some friends who considered themselves activists, yet in his estimation "they just argue and blog in coffee shops while the world burns around them. Better to close the laptops and go into the world than criticize everything in safety. Maybe put down that Americano so you have another free hand to pick up a shovel for digging a well."

While this might come off as a pretty brash reflection, there is some truth here as seen in Job's actions. Being made for work means that we are called to do something about the suffering in the world. We are shaped for good works as a response to the pain around us. As we learn in Genesis, what it means to be human includes being created for work that provides purpose for others and for God. From the creation narrative in Genesis to our current economic crises, the notion of what it means to work with purpose is a vexing issue. What type of work is pleasing to God? Am I doing what God wants me to do?

THE FIFTEEN-MINUTE BURRITO

I graduated from college with an English and psychology double major, and after a year of doing an internship I was in serious need of career counseling. One of my mentors recommended I do some informational networking and seek out people in careers I might be interested in. One direction I considered was law school, so I contacted an attorney in town who was recommended by a friend. We met at a small burrito stand near his law firm one afternoon, and I began to ask him questions.

After about fifteen minutes he started looking at his watch and said, "Can you excuse me for a minute? I need to make a phone call." He then took out his phone, dialed a number, let it ring, and left a short voicemail. "There," he said, "you just saw much of my day. I bill out hours in fifteen-minute segments and need to be hitting a number daily and weekly for billable hours for the firm. One phone call to a client is a fifteen-minute block that can be billed for an hour. That call just bought lunch." He smiled and bit into his burrito.

We had a nice conversation. He shared about the ups and downs of his practice, things to consider in studying for the LSAT, and said he would be happy to meet again if I wanted to continue the conversation. But what stuck with me was the fifteen-minute billable hour I happened to be a part of and what it would mean to measure my life by billable hours.

I know a number of attorneys who have a clear sense of their work as a calling from God and give their time and energy for the forwarding of God's kingdom. Yet I also know that I was not formed as they were, and my calling is much different in both skill set and passion. I also know all too well the challenges of finding meaningful work in this world. We live in a time when people are brought under the weight of unemployment and underemployment that is spiritually, economically, and socially degrading. Rather than some proof statement that work itself is suffering, this condition shows how our call to purposeful work has been stripped away for many people due to the brokenness and sin of the world. Systems of injustice that prevent access to meaningful work is the issue, not work itself.

REAL FAITH: OFF-ROADING FROM THE
HIGHWAY OF CAUSE AND EFFECT

Another way that our calling to work gets twisted by the accuser is to see work as both our savior and our sustainer, that by doing the right things, working hard, and earning enough our life will make sense. As we see in Job this is not the case. Job is being encouraged by his friends to follow the well-proven path of traditionalism in order to find God's favor. It is tempting in times of struggle and loss to go back to doing what had seemingly brought our joy and happiness in order to find joy and happiness in our present. Yet Job must seek God and not merely a predictable path. Sometimes seeking after God and the meaning of our life will require taking not a well-paved highway but perhaps going off-road, which requires imagination, courage, and faith.

In Luke 22, as Jesus gathers his disciples together in the upper room and institutes the Eucharist or Communion, he does so through binding himself to the Passover as its source and substance. "*This* is *my* body, which is given for you. . . . *This* cup . . . is the new covenant in *my* blood" (Lk 22:19-20). He moves *into* the space of salvation for our world rather than being a spectator at a distance, and he calls the disciples to do the work as well: "Do this in remembrance of me" (v. 19). This kind of work—"do this"—is *poieite* in Greek, a word that resonates with our English term *poetry*. It's a deeply creative term, going to the heart of what it means for us to be God's people in dark and desperate times like ours: makers, doers, creators, just like the living God. Paul's letter to the Ephesians testifies to this reality too: "We are what [God] has *made* [*poiēma*] us, created in Christ Jesus for good works, which God prepared beforehand to be our way of life" (Eph 2:10). We are called to be people of work—work that is prepared in advance for us to do. And we are *not* called merely to wait for it to come to us. Instead, like Job, we need to have the courage to venture forth, risk failure, and meet the tasks God has for us in the places we least expect.

HONEST FAITH: WALKING TALL WITH A LIMP

Third, we have to accept the likelihood of our lives being in seasons of staggering and limping. When Jacob wrestles with God in Genesis 32, he asks for God's blessing, and God grants such a profound blessing that it forever disables Jacob both physically (Jacob's hip was dislocated, and he forever limped afterward) and spiritually (his name is forever changed: he is now Israel, "the one who has overcome") (Gen 32:22-32). To forge the path toward the places God has in store for us means risking who we are, who we have been, and even who we think we were meant to be. As Job chooses to go to where God is, the name of God that he evokes in Job 23:16 translated as "Almighty" is the root of *Shaddai*—the same name by which God had been known to Abraham, Isaac, and Jacob in Exodus 6:2-3. It was the ancient name of God, long before factionalism had begun to divide God's people into two kingdoms. In early translations of the Hebrew Bible into Greek, *Shaddai* was translated with the meaning "Almighty." The root word *shadad* can mean "to overpower" or "to destroy and remake," which would give *Shaddai* the meaning of "destroyer and maker" as well as "sustainer," representing one of the aspects of God, and in this context functioning essentially as an epithet.

To encounter God is to be destroyed in part: it is to lose part or all of ourselves so we can be remade. The God that Job seeks desires to destroy Job's sense of self-sufficiency because this God is sufficient to supply all of Job's needs—in other words, he's almighty.

FULL FAITH: WHEN ALL ELSE FAILS, EMBRACE HUMILITY

Finally, we have to accept the virtue of humility as what it means to be human, and suffering in this life will be one of our great teachers. Here I depart most completely from Dave Eggers's method. A brash sense of indifference and flippancy to the pain and suffering in the world will not see us through suffering. God calls us to a better way. As we see with Job, he is willing to submit himself to whatever God has in store, regardless of the outcome. As Job muses:

Today also my complaint is bitter;
    his hand is heavy despite my groaning. (Job 23:2)

His life has moved from objective, dispassionate reasonableness to the embodiment of questions framed as complaints (verbal and reasoned questioning of God's actions) and groanings (visceral and physical reactions to his loss and suffering that go beyond words and reason). In this way, Job has nothing left to lose at this point and yet still submits himself to following after God, even though he has no idea how to find the Lord. He has no GPS location, no map, no landmarks left, as we saw earlier:

If I go forward, he is not there;
    or backward, I cannot perceive him;
on the left he hides, and I cannot behold him;
    I turn to the right, but I cannot see him. (Job 23: 8-9)

He even muses rhetorically, "If only I could vanish in darkness, / and thick darkness would cover my face!" (Job 23:17), giving us the impression that if simply disappearing were an option, he would consider it. Yet Job knows that his story will not end in darkness, that it will be brought out into the light of the Lord: "For he will complete what he appoints for me; / and many such things are in his mind" (Job 23:14).

LAYING DOWN THE SELF, PICKING UP A LIFE

In this way, Job realizes through all his sorrows and losses and complaints and groanings that there is more to his life than merely building and sustaining a self—so much more. To focus on the self is to dive ever deeper into the void and hungers of our interior world. To build a life is to see our self as a well to be filled to overflowing, not merely for our own needs but to quench the thirsts and hungers of others and to irrigate the parched creation with the living waters of God. We need to find our self, and like Job this journey may be brutal and filled with sorrows. But to turn our self into a life requires making space for others and God to come into the labyrinthine depths of our heart and throw open the doors of our soul for the world to become a companion for the journey. The book of Job has a bittersweet ending: God does indeed respond to Job's complaints and groanings, yet Job does not receive back all that he lost. He has matured and been humbled in the presence of the God who can create and destroy but who loves and redeems. Job makes the summative reply to God in the beginning of chapter 42:

I know that you can do all things,
and that no purpose of yours can be thwarted.

"Who is this that hides counsel without knowledge?"
Therefore I have uttered what I did not understand,
    things too wonderful for me, which I did not know.
"Hear, and I will speak;
    I will question you, and you declare to me."
I had heard of you by the hearing of the ear,
    but now my eye sees you;
therefore I despise myself,
    and repent in dust and ashes. (Job 42:2-6)

CHOOSING A GUIDE OVER A MAP

The life that you will continually shape from this moment onward is ultimately not a memoir of your own life. It's *God's* story that you are participating in. It's that knowledge that moves Job out from beyond trying to locate God in the regions of reason alone, of divining the divine through restrictive maps of certainty or crass cynicism. What's needed in this life, as the story of Job shows us, is not a better map. Instead, after Job's example, it's time to risk laying down the maps from time to time, to listen to the God who alone is our Guide. In the end, Job's encounter with God will show that the maps we've learned to clutch don't actually depict the territory of freedom we think they do. Only El Shaddai himself can do that—and he calls us to let him take us there.

On their album *No Line on the Horizon*, the band U2 wrestles with a world in which the compass points of north, south, east, and west are harder to discern than ever before. Do we journey out into the wilderness, they ask—risking out hearts breaking, working yet again for something that might not gain us recognition and fame, possibly enduring pain and loss? In the song

"Stand Up Comedy," Bono proclaims—fire-and-brimstone Irishman that he is—that the time for sitting in the dust is over, and it's time to get out from under our beds and stand up for love. And while we are "getting over certainty," it's time to "stop helping God across the road like a little old lady."[6]

Job reminds us that we too need to stop trying to do it all on our own, to make our own way in the world, pretending that we have all the answers and offering a façade of self-sufficiency. Rather, in our heartbreak, loss, and sorrows, we need to ask the questions that still burn in our heart and step out in search for the Lord who will, like Job, meet us in the unexpected yet most intimate ways if we journey with faith and the humility to receive what is offered us. Are you ready to stand up and journey into the unknown? Are you willing to ask the hard questions in the darkness of this life and risk finding what the light of love might reveal in your life?

7

HOW CAN I BE BORN
AFTER GROWING OLD?

Questions About the Cost of Discipleship

Community cannot feed for long on itself; it can
only flourish where always the boundaries are
giving way to the coming of others from beyond
them—unknown and undiscovered brothers.

HOWARD THURMAN
THE SEARCH FOR COMMON GROUND

Finding authoritative sources that everyone can agree on has become a challenge in the twenty-first century. As my students work on research papers, they struggle with discerning which voice has authority on a subject in ways I never experienced when I was an undergraduate. Doing a search on a topic on Google will elicit thousands of hits providing sources that look and sound like the definitive word on a topic. At first glance it has become harder to tell what is a blog opinion from a university website, and many of the citations used to back up points of view are often merely commentary from an echo chamber of like-minded individuals with little to no external counterpoint. Even when people agree on some authority in their life, we often have varying interpretations as to what an authority says and asserts.

WHEN THE AUTHOR COMES TO THE CONFERENCE

At an academic conference in Dublin I was attending a few years ago, a number of scholars were gathering to reflect on the work of noted French philosopher Paul Ricoeur. While not necessarily a household name, Ricoeur's work has had a significant influence on the work of scholars in theology, literature, philosophy, economics, ethics, and political science. During the keynote panel discussion, a debate was underway in regard to the way in which one of Ricoeur's seminal works on narrative theory, *Time and Narrative*, was to be looked at in relation to Jewish texts written after the Holocaust. Given the gravity of the subject matter, it was becoming a heated debate among the panelists. Slowly there seemed to be a murmur arising from the audience and then heads started turning toward the back row. Paul Ricoeur, the philosopher himself, had slipped into the back row and had quietly taken a seat. No one knew he would be attending the conference, so this was a surprise to the say the least. As the panelists became aware of his presence, the former bravado and certainty of tone in their remarks fell away, and there were furtive glances between comments to the man in the row as if they were looking for some nod of the head or wink of the eye to assure them that their assertions regarding his work were indeed on track.

Toward the end of the debate, it was obvious that some statement needed to be made to acknowledge that the subject of the panel, let alone the entire conference, was seated in the auditorium! The chair took the microphone and acknowledged that Professor Ricoeur was in the room and wondered if he would like to make some statements related to the debate. As he was rather frail at this time, they brought a microphone to him. Professor Ricoeur took the microphone and simply said, "Everything I have to say has been written down. I just wanted to hear what you are doing with it now. Now is the season for the young to speak up. I have said my part." And with that he sat down. No one said a thing.

After the panel concluded, Professor Ricoeur slipped out the back as quietly as he had come in. Someone close to him later remarked that he simply heard about the conference and wanted to hear the discussion. Just curious, I suppose. But I am sure more than a few of us wished we had pressed him further. "Come, Professor, this is your work! Your words! Your ideas! Tell what the right way to approach it should be!"

I will admit that I feel the same way a lot of the time, especially when I struggle with questions I have in relation to faith in God. Perhaps you do as well. Don't you sometimes wish you could just grab some person out of history—say, the apostle Paul—and say, "Paul, tell 'em"?

Many of us have fantasies like that, especially around matters of faith. If we're honest with ourselves, many of us feel like the answer could be found if we could simply walk behind the popcorn counter, grab Jesus, pull him out, and say, "Would you please tell us what we're supposed to do? We're floundering around, we're praying, we're struggling. We just want to know! What are we supposed to do?"

Now that we have journeyed through some of the questions asked of God in the Old Testament, we're going to shift our focus to a few of the questions posed directly to Jesus and how they are instructive for us in our seasons of doubt and uncertainty. In particular, two encounters seem to sum up Jesus' teaching and ministry: the question of Nicodemus in John 3 and the question of the woman at the well in John 4. These questions draw from the work of God through the witness of faith we have followed via the Old Testament accounts of Cain, Abram, Moses, and Job. While there are many questions in the New Testament, we will spend the final chapters zeroing in on these two questions, in the hope of bringing our questions into alignment with the ministry and call of Jesus.

As we enter into the world of John's Gospel, it is important to underscore one point in particular: in order to see and hear the kingdom of God, we must live as people who are being continually reborn by the power of the Holy Spirit. Whereas when Cain, Abram, Moses, and Job spoke to God, many had to hide their faces for fear of death when the Lord spoke (see Ex 3:6), here in the New Testament the embodiment of Emmanuel, "God with us," means that an encounter with the living God in Christ and in Spirit becomes intimate and personal in ways that are distinct but not different from how the Old Testament characters encountered God. While the work of God is constant across the two testaments and the fullness of God has always been at work, the persons of Jesus and the Spirit bring a renewed *type* of presence: passionate binding between God and God's people as God uses the church for the sake of the world. Now God will use the body of Christ for his powerful, redemptive work. This commitment to the body of Christ as the place in which to find a deep relationship with God begins our narrative in relation to Nicodemus and the question that he poses to Jesus.

As we look into John 3, we hear the big question that Nicodemus asks Jesus. Nicodemus was lucky: he actually *did* get to keep the microphone in front of Jesus for further dialogue. Nicodemus, a teacher of the law, goes straight to the source, asking Jesus to step out and tell it how it is.

Among all the things that Jesus taught, New Testament scholars tend to lift up three sermons and teachings in particular to understand what Jesus was all about: the Sermon on the Mount (Mt 5–7; it's paralleled by the Sermon on the Plain in Lk 6); Jesus' announcement of his ministry as he reads the Isaiah scroll in Luke 4; and this passage in John 3 (extending into Jn 6), where Nicodemus asks the big question, "How can anyone be born after having grown old?" (Jn 3:4). Theologians throughout history have spent lots of time looking at what Nicodemus says to Jesus. In his commentary on the Gospel of John, Dale Bruner cites John Calvin as saying about this encounter that "their faith [Pharisees like Nicodemus] depended only on miracles and hitherto had no root in the Gospel, so that it could not be steady and permanent. . . . [This] passage should be observed carefully; not all who profess to be Christ's are such in His estimation."[1]

In the beginning of the passage, Nicodemus appears out of the shadows of night. He comes, apparently alone, to this meeting with Jesus. Yet in reality, like many of us, he's not truly alone because he has brought the entire tradition of the Hebrew people with him, along with the customs and commitments of the Pharisees, of which he is one. Just as you're bringing your heritage with you as you read these words, Nicodemus has brought his own past with him, along with the history of faith that formed him. It all works together in the background to frame the conversation.

When we looked at Moses in Numbers 11, we discussed the
fact that the burdens of our life will always come with us
wherever we go (see chap. five). One of those was the burden
of nostalgia, the past—constantly looking over our shoulders to
see where we come from.

Jesus doesn't speak well of the Pharisees in the Gospels. He
calls them "brood of vipers," "hypocrites," even "whitewashed
tombs" (see Mt 23:27, 33), using these names to describe the way
the Pharisees are trying to assert ownership over the essentials
of faith and make them their own. Dale Bruner, in a wonderful
commentary on the Gospel of John, has called the Pharisees the
"serious party." They are deeply, deeply serious about the borders
and boundaries by which faith can be preserved for the ages.

I have known many people who seek excellence and seriousness in what they do, and that's not a bad thing: people of
industry, people of influence, people who simply know the value
of good, hard work. In my life as a professor, I encounter undergraduate and graduate students who are deeply serious about
their studies and self-discipline. Athletes that I know, whether
they're into triathlons, marathons, swimming, soccer, or any
number of other sports, sacrifice immense amounts of time and
effort to meet goals for the competitions that they go out for.
Serious musicians practice for years to give us the gift of what
they do with seeming effortlessness. Each of us has benefitted
from someone's hard work, someone's self-control, pushing
themselves to their limits to give the world an excellent gift.

Being serious about excellence isn't a bad thing. This seriousness is something that is actually bringing Nicodemus to
Jesus in the first place. His pursuit of the truth has brought him
to Jesus' doorstep.

The Hebrew term from which we get the name Pharisee literally means "to be set apart." The Pharisees saw themselves as separate from the distractions that pull people away from essential faith. They didn't care much for distractions; they wanted the *important* questions answered. To do this, they would memorize a portion of the Torah (the teaching of Moses) so they could hold onto it for themselves and draw from it in their thinking anytime they wanted. In this way, they thought, they could truly engage the deep and important essentials of faith and not be caught up in the banal and ephemeral.

That's the level of "serious" that the Pharisees carried with them. This seriousness that brought Nicodemus to Jesus says a lot about what's going to happen next in the text. One way to think about Nicodemus is that he was a problem solver of the things of God, a kind of theological puzzle master. The world can be split into a lot of different categories of types of people. For example, some people are either Marvel Comics people or DC Comics people. Others are either *Star Wars* people or *Star Trek* people. There are people who are passionate about lemons or limes. Some people prefer cats over dogs. Still others are rabidly passionate about jigsaw puzzles or love crossword puzzles. Whatever the passion, people often have something they are passionate about and willing to sacrifice themselves to and even debate its worth to the bitter end. I have a relative who is passionate about collecting and working with various types of Rubik's cube puzzles. He will work and work and work with various strategies for hours to get all the colors on each side to match up.

Nicodemus is certainly a puzzle person of this intensity. He has a question in mind, a puzzle about God's character, and he's been able to get many of the pieces to fall into place, but he's missing a few crucial ones that will make the picture of God come into completion at last. Nicodemus thinks that Jesus is a piece of a larger puzzle he is seeking, and so he comes to him to ask for some wisdom.

But Nicodemus is about to find out that Jesus doesn't always fit into a theological puzzle, and he has a tendency to flip puzzle tables over in ways that Nicodemus might not expect. In Nicodemus's community, everything can be framed in the language of permission, of "What am I allowed to do?" and "What am I allowed to think?" It's no surprise, then, that Nicodemus starts out with a whole string of *can* questions as he approaches Jesus in John 3: "no one *can* do these signs that you do" (v. 2); "How *can* anyone . . . ?" (v. 4); "*Can* one enter a second time . . . ?" (v. 4); and later on, "How *can* these things be?" (v. 9). For Nicodemus, the whole puzzle is about what can or cannot be done.

Another way of putting this: he wants to know what the instruction manuals say. "How can I put the puzzle together in the way I have in my mind?" he might be asking. "I've got skills and willpower. I'm a serious person. I'm passionate. If I throw my back into it, anything can happen! So just tell me what I need to do, and I'll do it!" But what Nicodemus doesn't realize is the simple truth that anytime we focus on our capabilities, on our work ethic, on our willpower, the puzzle we're trying to construct is only going to be the size that we can imagine, no larger. But that's entirely too small for what God is trying to do. So when Jesus responds, he calls Nicodemus to lift his head up and above from the grand puzzle he seems to be working on and introduces an entirely new category: second birth.

"You must be born from above," Jesus tells Nicodemus (v. 7)—
or in another translation, "you must be born again" (NIV). The
Greek word here, *anōthen*, means "to lift one's face," to look up
from what one is doing, to see the heavens above as grander
than oneself. Jesus is calling Nicodemus out from the context in
which he's found himself, into a world much bigger than he's
ever known. Jesus isn't discounting the hard work that
Nicodemus has done as a serious or passionate person, as a hard
worker, not at all. His tools and his seriousness have gotten him
to this place, directly in front of the face of Christ. But they will
not get him the rest of the way on the journey. He's moving
outside of what he can do. The question is, will Nicodemus
allow himself to be called into what Jesus has in store?

My family and I enjoy watching nature documentaries. I love
learning about the amazing abilities that animals have, especially when they're under stress. When sharks are under stress,
for example, they swim at unbelievable speeds of up to twenty-
five miles per hour. When a cheetah is chasing something across
the Serengeti and running thirty, forty, or fifty miles per hour,
it's absolutely stunning to see, especially in slow motion. Then
it's poetry in motion.

What about human beings when we're under stress? Sometimes we retreat back into the things that we do well, but often
we just double down and do whatever we were doing before,
only twice as fast and twice as hard. Many of us become work-
aholics. If we have stress in our lives, we'll put our minds even
more deeply into what we're trying to do, as though that will
help us to punch through it. Some of us go to the gym and spend
hours and hours trying to break through what we're doing by
working it out through our bodies: lifting more, running faster,

moving with more fluidity. Some of us put in extra hours at work, spending unbelievable amounts of time at the office just to make ends meet. Some of us cram for hours and hours as hard as we can to get that grade that will allow us to pass the class.

These behaviors, on one level, may be acts of excellence, but they're still about "what I can do." They're all about *our* ability to get *ourselves* from point A to point B. But you know, point B is only the second point in a twenty-six-letter alphabet. There's a lot more beyond point B than Nicodemus has realized. That's where Jesus wants to take him.

DEAD MAN'S SHOES

I remember a time of working as hard as I could and seeming to get nowhere when I was serving as a minister in Scotland and was asked to visit a member of the congregation in the hospital, since he was in a coma and was dying. Charles was at the Canniesburn Hospital, which meant I needed to take the train from the university after my graduate seminar. It was already a long day, and once I got to the hospital and to his room, the ward Charles was on was completely quiet and deserted of other visitors, leaving only the night staff. He was in a coma, but I sat by his bedside and prayed for some insight as to what I needed to do.

The entire train ride I wondered what value I would bring by making the train journey; the man was in a coma, he probably couldn't hear and wouldn't know I was there. As a minister I believed deeply (and still do) in the power of prayer and the way God works beyond our actions. Yet at this moment I really didn't understand. I was tired. I was overwhelmed with graduate school. I was feeling alone and isolated in a country and culture far away from my home. And sitting by this man's bedside I was feeling worthless. I took out my Bible, read some psalms aloud, prayed, and after thirty minutes I left for the train station. Never before had I doubted my sense of calling to the ministry as much as at that moment. Nothing I could do seemed to change the status of the trauma this man was suffering. I did everything I was supposed to: I prayed, I read Scripture, I sat at the bedside. Yet when I left, Charles seemed to be unmoved and just as much in a coma as when I had arrived. It was as if my visit was nothing more than a rock thrown into the water. Once it struck the surface, the ripples died away and closed over any sense that I had been there. In all honesty, I felt defeated.

A month later I received a letter in the mail from a lawyer who represented the estate of the man in the coma. He had passed away and the family asked that I be remembered in his estate. When I called the family, they said that the nurses had told the family about my visit, and they wanted to say thank you for representing Christ by being present. In the letter the family gave me a check for twenty-five pounds. I just stared at it and had a rush of emotions but mostly felt shame. How could they give me anything? I knew in my heart how doubting and hesitant I was.

I had been doing everything "by the book"—working hard at the cathedral I was serving, life and research as a PhD student, focusing on my own walk with God. Yet I still didn't feel equipped to sit with this man in a coma, nor did I deserve this simple gift of thanks. I thought about sending it back, giving it away, or simply tearing it up. Yet I spoke with a friend who was a priest in Glasgow to get his opinion. "This check isn't about you, Jeff," he said. "This is about paying it forward beyond you.

For some reason what you did was more than you or your intentions, so you need to honor that somehow in his name."

His words spoke truth (as usual, those Holy Spirit Scots know how to speak deep into you) and I wrestled with what to do. Over the past year I had worn down the shoes I had brought with me to Scotland and, given the exchange rate, I hadn't purchased another pair. So while it might seem weird, I bought a pair of black Dr. Martens boots. I didn't have a car, so I walked all over the city on a regular basis. As I thought about "paying it forward beyond myself," I thought that perhaps I needed to memorialize every step I took as a minister in the name of Charles and what he taught me from his place in a coma. That faith sometimes takes you beyond what you ask for and inserts you in a place where you need to begin again, with a new pace and gait and purpose and stride that gives wind to our sails more than who we are and what we can accomplish alone.

Those tough-as-nails Dr. Martens carried me through research, graduate teaching, weddings, funerals, baptisms, and even into the delivery ward for my daughter's birth. Charles was always there, reminding me to have faith, to show up, and be ready for the unexpected.

WHEN IT'S NOT THE PUZZLE THAT GETS SOLVED BUT US

Jesus is calling Nicodemus to move beyond the horizons he knew before. Jesus is more than a puzzle to be solved. He himself is the context by which everything falls into place. The puzzle is actually *Nicodemus*. The piece that is missing is in his heart, not in his brain, not in his intellect, and Jesus pulls him in at this point by saying that Nicodemus has to be born again. It completely blows Nicodemus's mind. Jesus isn't trying to give him an easy solution to a brain teaser. He wants to give him a pathway to life everlasting—to set him free.

> "Very truly, I tell you, no one can see the kingdom of God without being born from above." Nicodemus said to him, "How can anyone be born after having grown old? Can one enter a second time into the mother's womb and be born?" Jesus answered, "Very truly, I tell you, no one can enter the kingdom of God without being born of water and Spirit." (Jn 3:3-5)

"Water and spirit"? A very interesting phrase! For Nicodemus, he's a bit confused by this, because he knows the water part already but not the Spirit part. Besides, ritual cleansing was very much a part of the practices of the day for Pharisees. "Water?" he might have said. "You've got to be kidding me! Come on— *baptism*? That's the best you've got?" Nicodemus would have been used to doing ritual cleansing for days on end every time he entered the temple. He understood what cleansing was about. It'd be like asking an Olympic runner to walk around the block at a leisurely pace or taking someone who lives in Seattle to a café and only ordering a plain, boring coffee. To Nicodemus, the bar here seems to be set way too low. There's got to be something more here that Jesus is expecting.

DON'T FORGET TO WASH BEFORE SUPPER

But here's what's happening: it's the water *coupled with Spirit* that changes everything, for the mundane parts of what he thinks of as ritual cleansing have been taken to a completely different level by adding the additional element of Spirit. Baptism has been part of religious traditions for almost as long as we can remember: it's in Homer's *Iliad*, for example, when Achilles gets dipped (*baptizō*) into the river Styx and gains the power to defeat his enemies. Baptism shows up in the Old Testament too: in Exodus 29, in Leviticus 17, and in Deuteronomy 21 we learn that baptism is cleansing and cleansing and cleansing.

But for Jesus, baptism is more than simply cleansing. Through the Spirit, he tells Nicodemus, the cleansing is going to make what was invisible *visible* to the kingdom. In baptism, we are bound to the Spirit of God in a way that to the world makes us seem like Jesus people. Here Jesus is fulfilling a prophecy from Ezekiel where God says, "I will sprinkle clean water upon you. . . . I will put my spirit within you, and make you follow my statutes and be careful to observe my ordinances" (Ezek 36:25, 27), and "I will put my spirit within you, and you shall live" (Ezek 37:14).

When we looked at Moses in Numbers 11 (see chap. five), we saw how the rabbis had wrestled for centuries to figure out what the essentials of Torah, of law, were about. Many of them landed on Habakkuk 2:4: "the righteous live by their faith." When Jesus describes being born of both water and Spirit, he recalls the prophecy of Ezekiel, which is essentially, "My spirit is going to be put in *you* so that you shall live. By my faithfulness, you shall live—not merely be clean, but actually have *life*." Furthermore, Jesus is calling Nicodemus not to stay in those waters forever. In John 3:5, as Jesus calls him out of the waters, he uses the word *ek*, "out of," to describe the relationship he wants Nicodemus to have with the water: "no one can enter the kingdom of God without being born of [*ek*, "out of"] water and Spirit." In essence, the passage is saying that Nicodemus's call—our call as believers in Jesus—is *to be born up and out of the waters, into the spirit of God, and out into the world.*

GET OUT OF THE WADING POOL: FINDING MORE THAN CERTAINTY BY FINDING COMMUNITY

That wonderful little preposition *ek* is the same one that is used to describe the community of faith. The New Testament word for the church is *ekklēsia*, (*ek* + *klēsia*)—those who are *called out* of the world to be sent back into the world to witness to the kingdom of God. Jesus wants Nicodemus to experience that kind of calling out, so he essentially says to Nicodemus, "Get out of the wading pool. Get out of the shallow end! You've waded into the waters for cleansing and ritual, but your feet are always on the pebbles of the beach. I want to draw you into the deep waters, away from the pebbly shore, so far out that being immersed in my love and coming back to life may be the best way to describe it." Nicodemus's world is flipping upside down, and baptism, as he's always understood it, is changing dramatically now that Jesus is binding it to the Spirit of God.

This is a challenging call for anyone, let alone Nicodemus, who has studied the Scriptures for years. The call to "get out of the wading pool" hits many people in different ways. For some, getting out of the wading pool and moving into the deeper waters will mean working through an abusive childhood trauma that has held them back from intimacy with others for years. For others, getting out of the wading pool might mean leaving behind seemingly safe job prospects and following a calling that God has placed on their heart for years, but they feared the economic and social uncertainty. Getting out of the wading pool might mean acknowledging some subtle yet deep prejudice and submitting to a new racially diverse community of faith to build trust and reconciliation.

THERE'S ALWAYS ROOM FOR ONE MORE IN HACKY SACK AND FAITH

A good friend of mine had a "get out of the wading pool" moment when he returned from Iraq. Having served in the Marines for two tours of duty, Steve was the first to admit that he returned stateside pretty shattered, broken in heart and soul. He loved the Lord, prayed and read his Bible regularly, but couldn't connect with the churches he tried to get involved in. It was like he brought back a dark cape that blocked his heart from others, and the chill of that shade made it difficult to be around other people.

One day he was walking through a park in Seattle and saw a group of men playing Hacky Sack. These guys were kicking a Hacky Sack bag around the circle in the sunshine, laughing, and poking fun at each other in their mutual lack of skill. As Steve walked by he noted that there was "something different" going on with them, that this simple, silly game had more going on than he could describe. All he knew was that he wanted to go over and say hello. At an even deeper level, he remembers thinking that these men could somehow bear the weight of all that was broken and twisted inside, that in their laughter there was something unforced and free. Not the cynical and ironic laughter that you hear with casual acquaintances or coworkers trying to impress each other. No, this was a free, light laughter. And in ways he couldn't describe, he knew it was real, like the sun and wind and sea are real yet defy full explanation. But something real can be blinding, and it was as if Steve's feet were locked for a minute. He was not sure what to do.

As he stood there in that moment of confusion, one of the young men just called out, "Hey! Come on over! Wanna play?" As these now friends of thirty years tell this seemingly mundane encounter, something (or in the truth of faith—Someone) told them to open the circle and invite Steve's broken heart into the Hacky Sack game. Steve walked over, introductions were made, they kicked the sack a bit more, laughter started flowing again, and they went out for pizza.

Steve could have stayed where he was. In his hurt. In his loss. In his pain. Yet the call to "get out of the wading pool" gripped him, and the circle of friendship opened for him. The journey these men have taken together over the years reads like an epic: marriages, loss of children, bankruptcy, loss of faith, faith reborn, cancer, healings, funerals. Yet through it all these men have continued to swim deeper and deeper into the waters of fellowship one stroke at a time, never looking back.

"Baptism is in the New Testament in every case the indispensable answer to an unavoidable question by a man who has come to faith," wrote the theologian Karl Barth. "In the sphere of the New Testament one is not brought to baptism; one comes to baptism."[2] Elsewhere, Barth writes that

> baptism needs neither repetition nor over-emphasis. . . . The praise of God is the theme of each new day, each new hour. The glory of baptism among all parts of the Church's proclamation is its "once-for-all-ness." For Jesus Christ died once for our sins and awakened once from the dead for our justification [*ephapax*/ἐφάπαξ, "once for all"].[3]

Romans 6:10, Hebrews 7, and Hebrews 10 all speak about Jesus's sacrifice as a once-and-for-all-time act. Nicodemus is to be finished with the cycle of cleansing, of only standing up to his knees in the water of grace, never fully committing to the full life that is being offered him. Jesus is inviting him to go out to the deep, to be brought out to a place where his own will-power and his own "can" won't be enough. He will have to rely on Jesus and his Spirit to pull him deeper and deeper.

Galatians 3 says that in the life of grace, "there is no longer Jew or Greek, there is no longer slave or free, . . . for all of you are one in Christ Jesus" (Gal 3:28). Many of the church's early converts were former slaves, people of poverty, illiterate, or widows or orphans seeking a place to call their own. The church promised a place to belong—exciting news for someone who has nothing to lose and everything to gain. But for someone like Nicodemus, a Pharisee who has been educated at the top rung of teaching and has social status and power, following Jesus means giving up any sense of self-sufficiency he may have developed in order to plunge totally into God's power and providence. It no longer matters in the same way whether Nicodemus is a priest or not, whether he sits in the inner circle of Jewish leadership or not, whether he has climbed up the social ladder, has worked to get his kids into the right schools, has put a down payment on a house in the right neighborhood, or has bought the luxury car. All that matters for Nicodemus is that he binds his life to Jesus instead of to the life he has built for himself.

LIFE IS SUFFERING, NOT WITH A PERIOD BUT A COMMA

It is important at this point to underscore that there are some questions we will never get to the bottom of or feel like we have peace with in this life. When Jesus tells us to expect "wars and rumors of wars" and that "the poor will always be with us," it is an acknowledgment that suffering and pain are part of this broken and battered world. A key point of all world religions is that suffering is real. Children are abused. Economic injustice is real. Racism continues to rear its ugly head and scream its cries day after day. Gender inequality and sexual violence continue to plague society. Power is wielded dispassionately, and the marginalized are continually silenced. When the psalmist muses, "Why do the nations rage?" (Ps 2:1 ESV), it is a cry from the depths of our souls that acknowledges this world is still horribly twisted in many ways and darkness seeps into everything. Yet here, in the ministry of Jesus, the reality of suffering and pain finds not merely necessary location but also the true Gardener who will help us to weed, prune, and train the twisted and battered limbs of the tree of life back to the place where it can once again bear fruit in the light of love. While it is right to acknowledge that "life is suffering," as most religions do, it is also vital to acknowledge that life is not only suffering—there is more. "Life is suffering" cannot be marked with the finality of a period, but through the ministry, cross, and resurrection of Jesus Christ, it is marked with a comma: life is suffering, yet there is still love.

The church father Gregory of Nazianzus stated in the early centuries of the church that "Christians are not known by their sickness, but by their cure." This truth is a challenge and testimony in the face of suffering that Nicodemus discovered. More than discovering the answer to *why*, he was challenged to redirect his questioning to *who*: Who can I bring the pain and loss of my life to? Who can bear the weight of this world's brokenness?

Who is able to reach deep enough into the darkness and still bring forth light? Who can make me whole after sexual violence? Who can bring my life together when my family falls apart?

The push for Nicodemus is not just that he has to bind his life to Jesus. He actually has to go a step further and bind his life to God's Spirit, which will mean changing and becoming new. For some people, that's easy—but it may not be easy for Nicodemus. "Very truly, I tell you," says Jesus, "we speak of what we know and testify to what we have seen; yet you [plural] do not receive our testimony" (Jn 3:11). Note the plurals in that verse. Who are the *we*s and the *our* Jesus is evoking? What's he talking about?

He's talking about the Jesus followers—the Jesus-testifying company of disciples that is around him at this time in his ministry. Jesus is pulling back the camera from a close-up to a wide-angle shot and saying, "Nicodemus, the friends and the people you surround yourself with now are going to have to include these people, my followers, too. When you walk out into the public, and people see you and talk about you, these people (Jesus' disciples) are your family. That's who we want you to be a part of now."

When I stop and think about the implications of Jesus' invitation, I have a *whoa* moment. It's one thing to go to work, to know that I am a Christian, to keep a Bible in my drawer, maybe mention it every once in a while. Those things are nice things, but I really want to stay over here, on the safe side of the social register. But Jesus is saying that's not possible. He's inviting Nicodemus—and us—to realize that his community includes people he never may have thought of. "You're saying that my family includes people in Costa Rica, Jesus? People in Russia? The poor *and* the rich? The disabled? The people in the neighborhood I just spent ten years trying to escape?" And Jesus says: *absolutely.*

The grand do-over that Nicodemus is being called into is more than just a reboot of his life. It goes deeper, to a level at which God is making a *people* of God—a community of God followers who are going to show the world that divisions no longer hold. The chasms between people driven by culture, poverty, and race are *false*, and God is raising up something new. Nicodemus now gets to be part of that story. He has gifts, he has talents, he has passions. He is serious. But is he serious enough to see where God is leading him?

Nicodemus's world is being completely inverted, but Jesus isn't quite finished. "Just as Moses lifted up the serpent in the wilderness," he goes on, "so must the Son of Man be lifted up, that whoever believes in him may have eternal life" (Jn 3:14-15). The verb used for "believes" here is a present-tense verb. Trusting is all that is requested of Nicodemus—and it's not trusting in belief but in the person of Jesus himself. "Do you trust not in philosophy, not in your memorization skills, not in your work ethic but in me, Nicodemus? When all the chips hit the ground, will you trust in me to lead you where I am going to take you, to the people I'm going to take you to, to the life I have in store for you? Will you simply trust me?" For Nicodemus, saying *yes* to Jesus' invitation is going to be a complete game changer.

"The righteous live by their faith" (Hab 2:4). We must turn our faces up from this puzzling world and learn to see what Jesus wants to call us to, not just for one time but for all time. Following Jesus means that your life is now different. Yes, it's going to cost you something to follow Jesus. He may take you to places that will scare you or make you feel out of your league.

He may put passion in your heart for something you maybe don't even know about right now, or he may cause you to learn to love people you can't yet imagine loving. But what Jesus calls you to will revolutionize your world and help you to see things as he does.

A little later in John's Gospel, Nicodemus makes another appearance, and by that point it's pretty clear he gets it. He understands what God has called him to and responds, and it awakens in him something he never knew was possible. What do you see Jesus calling you to right now? As you come out of the dark of night and face Jesus, are you trying to make him a puzzle, to make him into a piece to fit your world? Or are you allowing yourself to be remade and reborn, as Nicodemus was? What does it look and feel like when you catch a glimpse of what's possible in the kingdom of God? Is it something small, something that fits your can-do work ethic? Or is it something so vast, so impossible, that only God can make it possible? Is that what the kingdom of God is going to be like for you?

In a sense, the question for Nicodemus is the same question that I have asked repeatedly in this book: Where are you, right now (Gen 3:9)? Are you hiding in the shadows, or are you ready to come out and meet Jesus as he really is? Come out of the shadows. Come out of the wading pool and into the deep. That's where the action is. That's where the fullness of God is. That's where the living Christ is waiting to meet you. It may not be easy, but it will be real, and Jesus is inviting you to let him take you there.

If you are at a place in your life where you want to be reconciled with God, if you're are at a place where you are ready to get real with God and you feel a tug of the Holy Spirit on your heart, I'd like to invite you to kneel and pray and ask God to do a cleansing work in your heart and a binding work in your life. Maybe you've been walking with Jesus for a long time, but you don't know what the next step is. Maybe it feels like a leap over the edge of a cliff or a zip line ride from a telephone pole. Maybe this is the first time you've ever heard Jesus' call, and maybe today you want to make it a part of your life too—to say yes to his plan for you. If that's your story, take some time to come out of the shadows and into the light with Jesus.

8

WHERE CAN I GET
THAT LIVING WATER?

*Questions of Commitment
and Community*

*Scars have the strange power to remind
us that our past is real.*

CORMAC McCARTHY
ALL THE PRETTY HORSES

*Sin and grace, absence and presence, tragedy and
comedy, they divide the world between them
and where they meet head on, the Gospel happens.*

FREDERICK BUECHNER
TELLING THE TRUTH

If you've ever seen a postcard of the downtown Seattle skyline,
there's a good chance it was taken from Kerry Park. It's about
a mile from my university and has an incredible view: you can
see most of downtown Seattle, the ferry boats shuffling com-
muters into Elliott Bay and out to Puget Sound, and on a clear
day the impossibly majestic backdrop of Mt. Rainier. The park

itself is only a few meters across, but standing in the middle of the viewing area is a curious sculpture made of steel. It looks like a twenty-five-foot-tall rectangular box with a large oval taken out of each face, leaving huge openings that people can walk through and see the scenery on the other side. Conceived and built in 1969 by local artist Doris Chase, the sculpture is called *Changing Form.* I remember seeing that title for the first time and wondering what was supposed to be so changing about a huge piece of steel art. Then one day, as I happened past the sculpture on a walk, I realized the significance of the title. *Changing Form* isn't referring to the sculpture but to the view through the middle of it.

Over the years, my hometown has changed dramatically. Looking at old photos of my family standing at Kerry Park with the skyline in the background, it strikes me that many of the buildings standing today didn't exist in those days, like the imposing Columbia Center (which is the tallest tower in town, despite the way the Space Needle might look from the deceptive vantage of Kerry Park) or the 772-foot "Spark Plug" tower. In the time I've been married, two new sports stadiums, collectively hosting Seattle's football, soccer, and baseball teams, have been constructed; and an older stadium, the Kingdome, considered by many to have been one of the greatest sports arenas in America, has been torn down. The city itself, which looked so pristine when I was younger, I now know to be a complex place filled with commerce and culture I never knew would exist. Amazon, Starbucks, and Microsoft weren't even dreams when this sculpture was constructed, and now they and many other corporations not only fill the Seattle skyline but serve as the new frames by which people see the world.

THE TIMES THEY ARE A-CHANGIN'

We live in times of great change. The places we are from and
where we now live aren't the same places that we remember
them to have been long ago. You and I are the same way, constantly changing from season to season and year to year, devel-
oping, maturing, backsliding, making mistakes, learning to
thrive, figuring out what's most important to us. Change is a
part of our lives, sometimes for the better and sometimes for
the worse.

Sometimes we find that our beliefs are truer than we ever
realized, yet through questioning and testing them, we can find
even more grounding and go much, much deeper into what we
have found to be true. By asking questions of God, of each
other, and of our own understanding of how the world works,
we risk uncertainty and doubt, but we move closer to the intimacy and care that God has always desired for us—especially
if we prioritize relationships amid our questioning along the
way. The last thing the kingdom of God needs is another person
choosing to dine at the appetizer tray of isolation and ignorance
while the banqueting table of Scripture, reason, tradition, and
experience is sitting right before us, so rich and sustaining for
those who have ears to hear and eyes to see.[1] Questions asked
with integrity and humility before the Lord will bring us to the
banquet, but we still need to load up the plate and dine.

JESUS OFFERS A FRAME FOR OUR
QUESTIONS AND OUR FAITH

The gospel of Jesus Christ isn't meant to block our view of this
world with a pretty, gilded structure. Doris Chase didn't make
Changing Form opaque, and neither did the triune God of the

universe make his good news into something meant to restrict our view of what is true, real, and beautiful: he means to give us a *clearer* vision of what's possible in our lives and in the world. People are often hesitant to ask deep questions simply because they fear that the world will change for the worse if they get an answer they don't like or expect. But in truth, our faith can be a frame, like a sculpture, through which we can view this weary, broken, yet beautiful world—our neighbors near and far, the ideas that have been born throughout the centuries, the astonishing array of culture that God's Spirit has inspired across time and place—as part of the marvelous, awe-inspiring reality that is part of the kingdom of God.

In his poem "Poetry," Pablo Neruda describes this experience of having his view reframed. He begins describing being overwhelmed as the thought of poetry and writing poetry seems to come searching for him. His life was moving along with predictability when he was taken away from what was normal and "saw the heavens unfastened." He concludes by saying that in that moment it was as if he became "part of the abyss / I wheeled with the stars / my heart broke loose on the wind."[2]

Like being a pure part of the abyss, wheeling with the stars and having our heart broken free on the open sky, so too is the life of faith, when it brings the hard questions to the feet of Jesus to learn that it's a place of wonder and indescribable grace.

In John 4, one chapter after Jesus' chat with Nicodemus, the Lord moves into a dialogue with an unnamed woman of Samaria at a well. It recalls a story that would have been familiar to Jewish readers: the story of an important marriage with Rebekah and Isaac's representative, meeting at a well (Gen 24), leading to a lineage that resulted in the birth of Jesus and the salvation of God's people. Moses met his wife Zipporah at a well in Midian (Ex 2), and perhaps most famous of all, Jacob and his wife Rachel met at a well in Haran (Gen 29). Jesus' encounter with the woman in John 4 actually takes place at that very same well. The name for the surrounding area has changed—no longer Haran but Samaria—but the Jews would still have recognized the significance of Samaria as the Israel of long before. Samaria was the Israel of Jacob's day, before the people broke into divisions based on doctrine and where someone was born and the source of their ethnicity. This particular well represents such a time before all the brokenness took place—a "deep" well (Jn 4:11), going far below the surface of time and space, requiring work, effort, and attention in order to extract the water and the stories that it contains.

The encounter is also located in the middle of the Cana-to-Cana travels of Jesus—between his appearance in John 2 at the wedding of Cana, where he turns water into wine, inspiring his Jewish disciples to believe for the first time that he is the Christ, and ending in John 4 with the healing of the royal official's son in Cana. In the first miracle, Jesus' Jewish disciples believe; in the second, a non-Jew believes. Within this circle of going out from Cana and returning, the woman Jesus encounters at Jacob's well is also contrasted with the story of Nicodemus from John 3 (see chap. 7), when Nicodemus visits Jesus, after which Jesus disappears into the Judean countryside, leaving Nicodemus confused. In the John 4 encounter, however, the woman meets Jesus at high noon, accepts and believes Jesus' claim, and brings others to Jesus on the basis of her testimony. Through it all, the sign of the text and its placement encourages us to watch this encounter closely, to see it as central between the two book-ended visits to Cana.

UNEXPECTED ENCOUNTERS WITH GRACE

Over the past few years our university has hosted a portable, self-managed community of one hundred men and women experiencing homelessness. Their encampment, Tent City 3, is self-sufficient in that members set up and break down their encampment every ninety days, since they are regulated and can't stay in one location beyond three months. Eligibility to be in the community is based on a government-issued photo ID, and security workers are on duty twenty-four hours a day when the community is encamped on a host property. The community is democratically organized: all members vote on big decisions affecting everyone, and all members agree to live together with a strict code of conduct that requires sobriety, nonviolence, cooperation, and participation in caring for both the encampment and the land the host has provided.

While there is almost universal support of our partnership with the homeless community, each time Tent City 3 comes to campus there are questions from some students, parents, faculty, and the neighborhood surrounding us. Will this be safe? Will it be dirty? How can we be sure the people will respect the neighborhood? Moments like these show the stereotypes people have of homelessness and of those who are homeless. Just like any community, there are those who can cause problems. Yet over and over again, once the community comes, settles in, and we start to get to know each other on a daily basis, the questions fall away.

Stereotypes and prejudice often operate like an abstract painting seen at a distance. When we keep the subject at a distance we tell ourselves that what we see is nothing more than a mess, chaos, without order or reasonableness. Yet as we spend more time looking and listening, when we risk drawing closer and closer and see the strokes of the brush, the play of light on the canvas, the history and intentions of the artist, we can find spellbinding wonder and humility and perhaps even exclaim aloud, "How have I lived so long without you?" Such is it every year when our friends from Tent City 3 come to share life with us for ninety days.

Homelessness becomes not merely an issue for politicians but for Mark and Sarah and Larry and Big Rob and Gillian: people with stories of hurt, joy, success, failure, scars, and strength that teach so many about parts of the kingdom of God. I don't notice them when I am driving to work at thirty miles an hour and the world is only an abstracted blur outside my window. Real people with gifts, talents, passions, hopes, and dreams teach us about God and ourselves in ways we never can find if we stay in the shallow wading pool of the known and the predicable. These surprise encounters with grace happen repeatedly for our students during these visits, and they are forever changed as they see not merely a person on the sidewalk but a unique, unrepeatable miracle of God who has a vantage point and frame for the gospel we often don't have.

This is the type of encounter with grace we see as Jesus approaches this woman at the well. Readers and listeners might have a preconceived picture of who this Samaritan woman might be, but as we move closer and allow Jesus to frame the scene for us, things come into focus in new and powerful ways.

Earlier in John's Gospel, Jesus had revealed himself as the true bridegroom at the wedding of Cana, the one who would fulfill the richness and hope that is the deepest meaning of marriage. Jesus had also been identified by John the Baptist, who spoke of Jesus as the true bridegroom given by God to Israel as a bride (Jn 3: 27-30). This true Bridegroom comes to the deep well of ancient Israel in the full light of high noon, the time when the sun stands directly overhead and shines directly down, taking away all the shadows. Here, at this place and time, Jesus meets the woman of Samaria.

Like other symbolic characters in the New Testament—the beloved disciple (Jn 19), the royal official (Jn 4), the paralytic at the pool (Jn 5), the man born blind (Jn 9)—we are not given the name of this woman. She comes to represent not only one person in particular—a specific woman of Samaria—but also the embodiment of a community and of those often marginalized by empire: Samaria, a people put aside by the traditions of first-century Israel and not seen as part of the inner circle of true believers because of a long history of idolatry. That she is a woman is itself crucial, a point she raises with Jesus. The ministry of God has always found its voice and face across race, class, and gender, and Jesus' encounter here underscores that the gospel is written both in the masculine and feminine for all to hear and heed. By even talking to her, Jesus challenges her understanding of Jewish tradition, which would have looked with disdain upon speaking publicly with a woman, let alone sharing utensils with her (Jn 4:7).

Jesus even claims to be on par with Jacob by claiming to bear "living water" (Jn 4:10), overshadowing the importance of the water contained by this well that Jacob himself had cut into the earth long before. The woman stands in this story not only to represent herself, her individuality and particularity, but for the Samaritan people and Samaritan women in general. Theologian Kelly Douglas Brown puts it this way:

> Samaritan women were considered the most impure of all. Multiple narratives of power intersected on the bodies of Samaritan women—ethnic, gender, and cultural. Put simply, they represented, at once, an inferior "race," gender, and religion. In this regard, the relationship between Jewish men and Samaritan women was one of extreme opposition.[3]

Jesus doesn't ignore history. He acknowledges the infidelity of the Samaritan people, how they forsook the one true God and chose to follow multiple "husbands," and how the allegiance they now had wasn't even to their "true husband" (compare Jn 4:16-18). The woman doesn't deny this, and in fact acknowledges that only a prophet would make an observation like that (v. 19).

She then asks Jesus where one is supposed to worship in true faith (v. 20). Is it on the mountain? she asks, since Mount Gerizim was considered a holy mountain to the Samaritan people. Or is it in the city, since the holy city of Jerusalem was the center of faith for the Jewish nation? The question of the place of worship is a theologically astute one. It had a history of splitting the people of God into factions, each group claiming solidarity with a particular sacred place—Jerusalem for the southern kingdom, Bethel for the north—and creating exclusive collectives around those locales that people "not of the place" would have difficulty getting to without belonging to the in-crowd.

WHERE ARE YOU NOW? WORSHIP CHANGES EVERYTHING

Jesus, standing next to a well from ancient times that went deep beneath the surface, calls the woman's attention to truth deeper than she had previously let herself imagine. "The hour is coming," Jesus tells her, "and is now here, when the true worshipers will worship the Father in spirit and truth" (v. 23). The woman, knowing that Jesus is now speaking of the promised Messiah, says that if and when the Messiah comes, she will do just as Jesus is suggesting (v. 25). But Jesus' response cuts to the heart of the Jewish faith: When he says "I am he, the one who is speaking to you" (v. 26), he reminds us of the name that was spoken to a people in the desert through Moses long before. Jesus' "I am he," *egō eimi* in Greek, which can also be translated "I AM," is the same name God gave to Moses when he was standing at the burning bush: "Thus you shall say to the Israelites," God said all those centuries before, "'I AM has sent me to you'" (Ex 3:14). But now, the "I AM" in the flesh is standing beside a well that had been constructed before the people split into factions, offering living water to all who come—not to a place, but to himself: the "I AM."

Jesus radically changes the frame of the question and deepens it. Returning in a sense to our first question from Genesis— "Where are you?"—Jesus acknowledges that the woman is astute in asking about worship since ultimately worship will be the key to everything Jesus wants to offer. When Jesus shares that he is the one, rather than a place, that is to be worshiped, he is placing the frame in front of himself to state boldly, "Do you see me now?" Where we worship and the community we worship with can block the view Jesus is offering of himself as the place of true worship.

Having been a pastor in a number of churches, I can safely say that the community you bind your heart to will either confirm or deny who Jesus is and what Jesus is calling you to. I have seen wealthy congregations absolutely certain of their mission and vision as a community yet often blindsided by their built-in systems of prejudice and bias. I have seen small urban congregations make sweeping stereotypes of people who attend larger suburban congregations. I have listened to rural congregations speak about the loss of faith in city churches without ever visiting or speaking with those members. While the Samaritan women's question is indeed astute, Jesus is also showing her that where he is, is the place of worship. In the end, worship is ultimately about *who* not *where*.

This is the first of many times that Jesus will use "I AM" in John's Gospel. He'll use it to show that he is the one who brings the things of earth (bread, water, light, vines) and the things of heaven together in himself (Jn 6:35; 8:12; 10:9, 11; 11:25-26; 14:6; 15:5). But here, in this first utterance, Jesus is bringing together a people with their God—I AM, and you are—echoing the covenant made with by the Lord: "I will be your God, and you will be my people" (Ex 6:7; Jer 7:23; 11:4; 30:22; Ezek 36:28). "I am he," says Jesus, but the question remains: "Are you to be my people?"

WE DO NOT WORSHIP GOD FULLY IN ISOLATION

The woman fully realizes who this is standing before her, this scandalous rabbi declaring what Moses only reported, claiming to on the authority of Abraham's covenant. She returns to her people, and because of her testimony, the people "left the city and were on their way to him" (Jn 4:30)—not heading to the mountains, not heading to the holy city, not even going to the well—they are going to *him*, the person of Jesus, the "I AM" in their midst. By asking the question of where to find living water, the woman at the well challenges us to dig deep and find the source of life and love that runs like rivers under all things. It is a challenge to get to the heart of the matter, to look beyond the superficial and momentary and fuel our life by the water of life that Jesus gives—water that is infinitely more satisfying and sustaining than quick-fix, fast-food spirituality.

What water are you drawing to quench your thirst? Where are you finding the source of life right now? Perhaps it is time to take stock of where you are, which well you're drawing from, and accept the invitation to drink deeply of living water.

CONCLUSION

I Was Blind, but Now I See:
Next Steps for the Journey

Though I was blind, now I see.

JOHN 9:25

Daniel Taylor wrote a thoughtful book titled *The Skeptical Believer* in which he outlined key characteristics of those people willing to ask big questions. Here are three of those characteristics:

- *Risk*: a believer's hunger for meaning is stronger than the fear of being wrong

- *Openness*: to the unknown, unverifiable, mysterious, intuited, spiritual, imagined

- *Love of companions*: shared risks relate to shared pleasure; kindred spirits[1]

As you have journeyed alongside the various people in Scripture asking big questions, the characteristics of risk, openness, and love of companions have been apparent in a variety of ways. From Cain to Abraham to Moses to the woman at the well in John's Gospel, we find risk, openness, and love of companions are all common threads. And it isn't just one question that makes our faith and life deepen. Rather, the story of faith is seen as a constellation of questions asked of God and others, providing a map to guide us in our journey. Like ancient mariners of the sea, we will find our truest path by a constellation rather than merely one light in the sky.

Throughout *The Skeptical Believer*, Taylor makes some assertions about the importance of questions that provide a good summary for your consideration as your look to the constellation of questions that are guiding you in your own story of faith. I have paraphrased ten assertions as follows.

TEN ASSERTIONS ABOUT LIVING THE QUESTIONS AS THE STORY OF FAITH

1. Asking questions is more compatible with faith than certainty is.

2. Like tolerance, doubt is not in itself automatically a good or bad thing. Sometimes doubt shows that you take truth seriously enough to dig deeper.

3. God is okay with our questions, and God also asks questions of us.

4. All explanations of the world are limited. Whether constructed from presuppositions, logical reasoning, or weighing and assessing the strength and significance of evidence, there is always more to discover.

5. The most important decisions in life, and the actions that flow from them, are made in light of imperfect knowledge. Every relationship begins with knowing enough rather than knowing everything.

6. The life of faith is compatible with doubt and intense questioning. It is not compatible with paralysis, indifference, or self-indulgence.

7. Religious faith can be defended rationally, but its truthfulness cannot be proved within human rationality. The same is true for secular faiths (in reason, science, political and social movements, etc.).

8. A number of people can end up with soul weariness from staying too long in questions. "Soul weariness" for Taylor is the condition that results from being hyper-reflective about something of great value with no definitive way of coming to a certain conclusion and no requirement to do so. Moving your questions into relationships, sharing them with close friends, helps to avoid seasons of soul weariness.

9. We should be realistic about what kind of answers to expect for certain kinds of questions. Different questions elicit different categories of answers. As you journeyed through *Live the Questions*, you saw how different questions brought forth different insights.

10. It is not a matter of choosing between exercising faith or not exercising faith in this life. It is only a question of what you will put your faith in, and faith is ultimately a love story. To quote Bob Dylan: "You're gonna have to serve somebody," so be considerate, thoughtful, and intentional about what and who you love.[2]

QUESTIONS THAT LEAD TO THE LIGHT:
JOHN 9 AND THE MAN BORN BLIND

In the New Testament, few people embody these points better than the man in John 9 who had been born blind. Light is one of the most widely used images in religions around the world and affirms the human desire for God. The use of light is significant in John's Gospel. Among the seventy-three New Testament occurrences total, there are twenty-three occurrences in John's Gospel and six in the book of 1 John. Light is characteristic of epiphany narratives (see Mt 17:2; Acts 9:3; 22:6, 9, 11; 26:13). Light is also represented in the divine power of God's liberation of captives (Acts 12:7; 16:29). In portraying God as one who "dwells in unapproachable light," 1 Timothy 6:16 employs the image of light as one of Judaism's traditional attributes of God.

The categories of light and darkness belong to a ubiquitous language of world religions. For example, Gnosticism, which developed in the dualistic systems of Manichaeism and Mandaeanism, was in effect a "religion of light" in which light and dark were seen as independent, opposing powers. While the use of the image of light and dark is seen as appealing to the author's formerly pagan readers, the image of light in the Old Testament is used in an intellectual sense to show truth and darkness as error and evil. Paul would therefore have spoken to a Jewish audience as well as a Hellenistic one.

As Jesus approaches the man born blind in John 9:5, he says: "As long as I am in the world, I am the light of the world." John's Gospel is filled with Jesus identifying himself as the "I AM" of Exodus 3:14. In John 9 the "I AM" is the *light* of everything—not merely the world but the entire universe! This grand light of faith, giving meaning to everything and making everything make sense, encounters the man who has never seen with his own eyes and now can.

When studying New Testament Greek, one of the first words students learn is the word for seeing or sight, which is *blepō*. In part it is because "to see" is so prevalent throughout the New Testament that they feel like they are getting somewhere. Jesus *blepōs* the man, and he now sees. But he not only sees: he also *testifies* to the fact that he can see, acting as a placeholder for Jesus in front of other people. In John 9:9, when people see the man, he is no longer begging, and they wonder whether he is the one they knew as "the blind man." He states rather resolutely that not only *was* he the one born blind, he is now the "I AM," albeit in a representative way. The Greek in the verse is translated in the NIV as "He himself insisted, 'I am the man.'" In actuality, as grammar geeks will point out, there is no object for the subject of the sentence: he only says "I am," which is one way of saying that he isn't defined by anything anymore. He is not "Formerly Blind Guy," nor is he even merely "Healed Guy." No, he is "I AM" in their presence. No more labels, no more using the compass points of culture to make sense of what is valued and what isn't: no, the encounter with Jesus so radically shifted the man that he simply was who he was, who he had always been meant to be: himself. I am that I am.

In the end, the man born blind cannot say what or how or why this miracle occurred. All he can offer, as we see in verse 25, is that "Though I was blind, now I see." As this section of Scripture closes, the man is thrown into the street, where Jesus (now thirty verses after the healing of the man's sight, making this the longest passage in the Gospels where Jesus is completely absent) shows up and asks if the man has faith. In verse 35, Jesus asks him, "Do you believe [*pisteuō*, "have faith"] in the Son of Man?" The man replies that he wants to have faith, but he doesn't know where to put it yet: "Who is he, sir?" the man asks. "Tell me, so that I may believe [*pisteuō*] in him." Jesus lays the cards on the table in verse 37: "You have seen [*blepō*] him, and the one speaking with you is he." The man replies, "Lord, I believe [*pisteuō*]," and he worships him (v. 38).

What is missing from this powerful exchange is a clear, concise articulation of what faith actually means in the form that is often spoken of in many churches. This is not a passage for people seeking after certainty and certitude. Jesus is absent for a long time, and the man is only left with his experience of an encounter. For the Gospel writer, this story is worthy of an entire chapter of text. No adherence to a particular doctrine, no perfunctory liturgical strategy, no catechism nor membership class to seal the deal: something *happened*. The man had faith in it. He knew one basic thing: that his life would never be the same. Jesus showed up, the man's life changed forever, and the Savior was worshiped.

The canon of Scripture holds this to be a sacred moment. Like with the many questions we have encountered in this book, the steps toward meaning in life require risk, faith, and the companionship of others—particularly trust in the living God— rather than answers that close off the need for risk, faith, and community.

Choosing a life of questions doesn't mean never coming to conclusions. It is, however, the path by which we always leave open space for new insights, new discoveries, and new relationships. Rather than certitude, good questions build confidence to trust and risk for the sake of love and meaning beyond our own understanding. There is so much to discover and deepen, and asking good questions is a spiritual discipline to help us get to where the light of love is waiting.

ACKNOWLEDGMENTS

Much of this book was framed and forged in the space of two loving communities: the university and the church. Over the decades I have found that some of the best questions that have led to deep faith came from dwelling in both the academy and the congregation. Akin to a generous and sanctified Venn diagram, the space created in the overlay of church life and academic life is where much of my sense of calling and responsibility has been given clarity and commissioning. For years I tried to live in one or the other, but my truest home is in the space between and betwixt these worlds, and for that I am so grateful.

This book began with a conversation among the pastors of Bethany Community Church in Seattle when I was graciously invited to serve as their preaching pastor for a season. I had been away from pastoral ministry for a while, and they gave me the collective grace, empowerment, prophetic insight, and humility to listen anew to the big questions of Scripture. Standing beside these men and women for a season on pastoral staff—and the beautiful family that is the church—reminded me of the gift that is the local church in such a complex and confusing age.

While the questions began life with the members of the church, the pruning and harvesting of these questions occurred in the classroom with the students at Seattle Pacific University as well as my time as a visiting lecturer at Blackfriars Hall Oxford, Fuller Seminary, Northwestern College, and Pepperdine University. My thanks to my students for pressing harder into difficult questions and especially to my colleagues in the School of Theology at Seattle Pacific University, who have always put first matters of the gospel for the sake of the kingdom of God demonstrated in all manners of excellence. They have been quick to correct and encourage my journey when I get lost in scholarly blind alleyways and to shine a light on truth to lead me back home. I would also like to thank Scott Rodriguez and the tribe at Stoneway Crossfit. As a Level 1 Crossfit trainer among these committed athletes, I have seen how hard questions of the body and soul are vital to understanding the deep questions of the spirit. Few spaces have taught me what transformation and growth look like as have the many hours training alongside these members of my Crossfit community.

My particular thanks to John Harrell for his wonderful edits of an initial draft and his encouragement to include more pop culture references rather than less. Also thanks to Al Hsu and the team at InterVarsity Press for taking this manuscript from proposal through to reality. Their challenge to put more skin in the game with this project was challenging and took my reflections to a necessary honesty that I pray bears fruit for you.

NOTES

INTRODUCTION: THE POWER OF ASKING GOOD QUESTIONS

[1]George Eliot, quoted in Rosemary Ashton, *George Eliot: A Life* (London: Penguin, 1996), 239. This statement is from a letter to her friend Barbara Bodichon regarding the overly scientific approach to life seen in Charles Darwin's writings.

[2]F. Scott Fitzgerald, *This Side of Paradise* (New York: Scribner, 1920), 282.

[3]William Shakespeare, *Hamlet, Prince of Denmark*, in *The Complete Works of William Shakespeare*, Shakespeare Head Press ed. (New York: Barnes and Noble, 1994), 1.3.78-80.

[4]Søren Kierkegaard, *The Sickness Unto Death: A Christian Psychological Exposition for Upbuilding and Awakening*, Kierkegaard's Writings 19 (Princeton, NJ: Princeton University Press, 1988).

1 WHERE ARE YOU?

[1]Sherry Turkle, "Always-On/Always-On-You: The Tethered Self," in *Handbook of Mobile Communication Studies*, ed. James E. Katz and Manuel Castells (Cambridge, MA: MIT Press, 2008), 121-38.

[2]Annie Dillard, *An American Childhood* (New York: Harper & Row, 1987), 45-48.

2 AM I MY BROTHER'S KEEPER?

[1]Dallas Willard, *Renovation of the Heart: Putting On the Character of Christ* (Colorado Springs, CO: NavPress, 2002), 35.

[2]Abraham J. Heschel, *Between God and Man: An Interpretation of Judaism* (1959; repr., New York: Simon & Schuster, 1997), 109.

[3]R. N. Whybray, "Genesis," in *The Oxford Bible Commentary*, ed. John Barton and John Muddiman (Oxford: Oxford University Press, 2001), 44.

[4]John Calvin, *Institutes of the Christian Religion*, trans. Henry Beveridge (1560; Peabody, MA: Hendrickson, 2008), 1.11.8.

[5]Willard, *Renovation of the Heart*, 36.

[6]Antoine de Saint-Exupéry, *The Little Prince*, trans. Katherine Woods (1943; repr. San Diego: Harcourt Brace Jovanovich, 1982), 9-13.

[7]Saint-Exupéry, *Little Prince*, 58-59.

[8]Saint-Exupéry, *Little Prince*, 64-71.

[9]Emmanuel Lévinas, *Ethics and Infinity: Conversations with Philippe Nemo*, trans. Richard A. Cohen (Pittsburgh: Duquesne University Press, 1985).

[10]Augustine of Hippo, cited in Charles N. Cochrane, *Christianity and Classical Culture* (New York: Oxford University Press, 1957), 403.

[11]Nathaniel Hawthorne, *The Scarlet Letter*, 1850.

[12]J. K. Rowling, *Harry Potter and the Sorcerer's Stone* (New York: Scholastic, 1997), 1.

[13]Walter Brueggemann, *The Bible Makes Sense*, rev. ed. (Winona, MN: Saint Mary's Press, 1997), 53.

[14] Edward Zwick, dir., *Blood Diamond* (Los Angeles: Warner Bros. Pictures, 2006).

3 HOW WILL I KNOW?

[1]Julia Baird, "Doubt as a Sign of Faith," *New York Times*, September 25, 2014.

[2]Neil Gaiman, *American Gods* (New York: William Morrow, 2001), 477.

[3]Gaiman, *American Gods*, 123.

[4]Baird, "Doubt as a Sign of Faith."

[5]J. K. Rowling, *Harry Potter and the Prisoner of Azkaban* (New York: Scholastic, 1999), 194.

4 WHO AM I?

[1]Brevard S. Childs, *The Book of Exodus: A Critical, Theological Commentary* (Philadelphia: Westminster, 1974), 73.

[2]Paul Auster, *Auggie Wren's Christmas Story* (New York: Henry Holt, 2004), 4-5.

[3]Auster, *Auggie Wren's Christmas Story*, 6.

[4]Auster, *Auggie Wren's Christmas Story*, 9.

[5]Dietrich Bonhoeffer, *Life Together* (New York: Harper & Row, 1954), 99.

[6]Marilynne Robinson, quoted in Wyatt Mason, "The Revelations of Marilynne Robinson," *New York Times Magazine*, October 1, 2014, www.nytimes.com/2014/10/05/magazine/the-revelations-of-marilynne-robinson.html.

[7]Eric Pianin, "10,000 Boomers Turn 65 Every Day. Can Medicare and Social Security Handle It?" *Fiscal Times*, May 9, 2017, www.thefiscaltimes.com/2017/05/09/10000-Boomers-Turn-65-Every-Day-Can-Medicare-and-Social-Security-Handle-It.

[8]Childs, *Book of Exodus*, 75.

[9]Martin Buber and Franz Rosenzweig, *Scripture and Translation* (Indianapolis: Indiana University Press, 1994), 138.

[10]Paul Tillich, "You Are Accepted," sermon 19, in *The Shaking of the Foundations: Sermons Applicable to the Personal and Social Problems of Our Religious Life* (New York: Charles Scribner, 1948), 161-62.

[11]Brevard S. Childs, *Old Testament Theology in a Canonical Context* (Philadelphia: Fortress, 1985), 36.

5 WHY THIS BURDEN?

[1]Eugene B. Borowitz, "Who Is a Good Jew?" in *Introduction to Judaism: A Sourcebook*, ed. Stephen J. Einstein and Lydia Kukoff, rev. ed. (New York: UAHC Press, 1999), 262.

[2]Daniel J. Levitin, *This Is Your Brain on Music: The Science of a Human Obsession* (New York: Dutton, 2006).

[3]The Head and the Heart, "Down in the Valley," *The Head and the Heart* (Seattle: Sub Pop Records, 2011).

[4]"Malawi Urges National AIDS Test," *BBC News*, July 16, 2007, http://news.bbc.co.uk/2/hi/africa/6900488.stm.

[5]C. S. Lewis, *The Problem of Pain* (1940; repr., San Francisco: HarperSanFrancisco, 1996), 93-94.

6 HOW CAN I JUST VANISH IN DARKNESS?

[1]Dave Eggers, *A Heartbreaking Work of Staggering Genius* (New York: Vintage, 2000).

[2]C. S. Lewis, *The Screwtape Letters* (1942; repr., New York: Macmillan, 1961), 60.

³Karl Marx, "Critique of Hegel's 'Philosophy of Right'" (1843; repr., Cambridge: Cambridge University Press, 1990), 8.

⁴Henry Wadsworth Longfellow, "I Heard the Bells on Christmas Day," 1863.

⁵Augustine of Hippo, *Confessions*, trans. R. S. Pine-Coffin (Baltimore: Penguin Books, 1966), 1.1.21.

⁶U2, "Stand Up Comedy," *No Line on the Horizon* (Universal Island Records, 2009).

7 HOW CAN I BE BORN
AFTER GROWING OLD?

¹Frederick Dale Bruner, *The Gospel of John: A Commentary* (Grand Rapids: Eerdmans, 2012), 170.

²Karl Barth, *The Teaching of the Church Regarding Baptism* (1948; repr., London: SCM Press, 1956), 42.

³Barth, *Teaching of the Church*, 64.

8 WHERE CAN I GET THAT LIVING WATER?

¹The fourfold formulation of Scripture, reason, tradition, and experience has been known in recent generations as the "Wesleyan Quadrilateral," a term coined by Albert C. Outler. For further elucidation of this idea, see Albert C. Outler, "The Wesleyan Quadrilateral—In John Wesley," in *The Wesleyan Theological Heritage: Essays of Albert C. Outler*, ed. Thomas C. Oden and Leicester R. Longden (Grand Rapids: Zondervan, 1991), 21-37.

²Pablo Neruda, "Poetry," in *Pablo Neruda: Selected Poems*, ed. Nathaniel Tarn, trans. Anthony Kerrigan, W. S. Merwin, Alastair Reid, and Nathaniel Tarn (1970; Boston: Houghton Mifflin, 1990), 457-59.

³Kelly Douglas Brown, *Stand Your Ground: Black Bodies and the Justice of God* (Maryknoll, NY: Orbis Books, 2015), 171.

CONCLUSION: I WAS BLIND, BUT NOW
I SEE: NEXT STEPS FOR THE JOURNEY

¹Daniel Taylor, *The Skeptical Believer: Telling Stories to Your Inner Atheist* (St. Paul, MN: Bog Walk Press, 2013).

²Bob Dylan, "Gotta Serve Somebody," *Slow Train Coming* (Columbia Records, 1979).

BIBLIOGRAPHY

"Apple Releases Brief, Fleeting Moment of Excitement." *The Onion*. September 9, 2014. www.theonion.com/apple-releases-brief-fleeting -moment-of-excitement-1819576902.

Augustine of Hippo. *Confessions*. Translated by R. S. Pine-Coffin. Baltimore: Penguin Books, 1966.

Auster, Paul. *Auggie Wren's Christmas Story*. New York: Henry Holt, 1990.

Baird, Julia. "Doubt as a Sign of Faith." *New York Times*, September 25, 2014.

Barth, Karl. *The Teaching of the Church Regarding Baptism*. 1943. Reprint, London: SCM Press, 1956.

Bonhoeffer, Dietrich. *Life Together*. New York: Harper & Row, 1954.

Brueggemann, Walter. *The Bible Makes Sense*. Rev. ed. Winona, MN: Saint Mary's Press, 1997.

Buber, Martin, and Franz Rosenzweig. *Scripture and Translation*. Indianapolis: Indiana University Press, 1994.

Calvin, John. *Institutes of the Christian Religion*. Translated by Henry Beveridge. Peabody, MA: Hendrickson, 2008.

Childs, Brevard S. *The Book of Exodus: A Critical, Theological Commentary*. Philadelphia: Westminster, 1974.

———. *Old Testament Theology in a Canonical Context*. Philadelphia: Fortress, 1985.

Cochrane, Charles N. *Christianity and Classical Culture*. New York: Oxford University Press, 1957.

Dillard, Annie. *An American Childhood*. New York: Harper & Row, 1987.

Douglas, Kelly Brown. *Stand Your Ground: Black Bodies and the Justice of God.* Maryknoll, NY: Orbis Press, 2015.

Eggers, Dave. *A Heartbreaking Work of Staggering Genius.* New York: Vintage, 2000.

Einstein, Stephen J., and Lydia Kukoff, eds. *Introduction to Judaism: A Sourcebook.* Rev. ed. New York: UAHC Press, 1999.

Fitzgerald, F. Scott. *This Side of Paradise.* New York: Scribner, 1920.

Gaiman, Neil. *American Gods.* New York: William Morrow, 2001.

Hawthorne, Nathaniel. *The Scarlet Letter.* 1850.

Head and the Heart, The. "Down in the Valley." *The Head and the Heart.* Sub Pop Records, 2011.

Heschel, Abraham J. *Between God and Man: An Interpretation of Judaism.* 1959. Reprint, New York: Simon & Schuster, 1997.

Lévinas, Emmanuel. *Ethnics and Infinity: Conversations with Philippe Nemo.* Translated by Richard A. Cohen. Pittsburgh: Duquesne University Press, 1985.

Levitin, Daniel J. *This Is Your Brain on Music: The Science of a Human Obsession.* New York: Dutton, 2006.

Lewis, C. S. *The Problem of Pain.* 1940. Reprint, San Francisco: HarperSanFrancisco, 1996.

———. *The Screwtape Letters.* 1942. Reprint, New York: Macmillan, 1961.

Longfellow, Henry Wadsworth. "I Heard the Bells on Christmas Day." In *A Christmas Anthology of Poetry and Painting.* Edited by Vivian Campbell. New York: Woman's Press, 1947.

Marx, Karl. "Critique of Hegel's 'Philosophy of Right.'" 1843. Reprint, Cambridge: Cambridge University Press, 1990.

Mason, Wyatt. "The Revelations of Marilynne Robinson." *New York Times Magazine.* October 1, 2014. www.nytimes.com/2014/10/05/magazine/the-revelations-of-marilynne-robinson.html.

Neruda, Pablo. "Poetry." In *Pablo Neruda: Selected Poems.* Edited by Nathaniel Tarn. Translated by Anthony Kerrigan, W. S. Merwin, Alastair Reid, and Nathaniel Tarn. 1970. Boston: Houghton Mifflin, 1990.

Outler, Albert C. "The Wesleyan Quadrilateral—In John Wesley." In *The Wesleyan Theological Heritage: Essays of Albert C. Outler*. Edited by Thomas C. Oden and Leicester R. Longden. Grand Rapids: Zondervan, 1991.

Pianin, Eric. "10,000 Boomers Turn 65 Every Day. Can Medicare and Social Security Handle It?" *Fiscal Times*, May 9, 2017. www.thefiscal times.com/2017/05/09/10000-Boomers-Turn-65-Every-Day-Can -Medicare-and-Social-Security-Handle-It.

Rowling, J. K. *Harry Potter and the Prisoner of Azkaban*. New York: Scholastic, 1999.

———. *Harry Potter and the Sorcerer's Stone*. New York: Scholastic, 1997.

Saint-Exupéry, Antoine de. *The Little Prince*. Translated by Katherine Woods. 1943. Reprint, San Diego: Harcourt Brace Jovanovich, 1982.

Shakespeare, William. *Hamlet, Prince of Denmark*. In *The Complete Works of William Shakespeare*. New York: Barnes & Noble, 1994.

Taylor, Daniel. *The Skeptical Believer: Telling Stories to Your Inner Atheist*. St. Paul, MN: Bog Walk, 2013.

Tillich, Paul. "You Are Accepted." In *The Shaking of the Foundations: Sermons Applicable to the Personal and Social Problems of Our Religious Life*. New York: Charles Scribner, 1948.

Turkle, Sherry. "Always-On/Always-On-You: The Tethered Self." In *Handbook of Mobile Communication Studies*. Edited by James E. Katz and Manuel Castells. Cambridge, MA: MIT Press, 2008.

Whybray, R. N. "Genesis." In *The Oxford Bible Commentary*. Edited by John Barton and John Muddiman. Oxford: Oxford University Press, 2001.

Willard, Dallas. *Renovation of the Heart: Putting on the Character of Christ*. Colorado Springs, CO: NavPress, 2002.

Zwick, Edward, dir. *Blood Diamond*. Los Angeles: Warner Bros. Pictures, 2006.